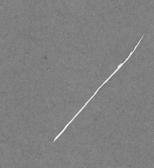

THE GREAT DINOSAUR ATLAS

Written by William Lindsay

Illustrated by Giuliano Fornari

Julian Messner

DK

A DORLING KINDERSLEY BOOK

Art Editor Penny Britchfield
Project Editor John C. Miles
U.S. Project Editor Nancy Furstinger

Designer Richard Czapnik
Editor Vicky Davenport
Production Teresa Solomon

Senior Editor Angela Wilkes
Art Director Roger Priddy

Published by Julian Messner, a division of Simon & Schuster,
Simon & Schuster Building, Rockefeller Center,
1230 Avenue of the Americas, New York, NY 10020

Julian Messner and colophon are trademarks of
Simon & Schuster, Inc.

Lindsay, William.
The great dinosaur atlas / William Lindsay: illustrations by
Giuliano Fornari.
p. cm.
Summary: A guide to the prehistoric world of dinosaurs
with maps, artwork, text, and pictorial spreads on the
reconstruction of a dinosaur.
1. Dinosaur - Pictorial works - Juvenile literature.
[1. Dinosaurs.] I. Fornari, Giuliano, ill. II. Title.
QE862 . D5L53 1991
567 . 9' 1 - dc20
ISBN 0 - 671 - 74479 - 8 (LSB)
ISBN 0 - 671 - 74480 - 1 (trade)   91 - 2838
                                                       CIP
                                                        AC

CONTENTS

Reproduced in Singapore by Columbia Offset
Printed and bound in Italy by New Interlitho, Milan

FACE-TO-FACE

MORE THAN 210 MILLION YEARS AGO, when Africa was joined to the Americas, and India was separated far from Asia, a new group of animals appeared on Earth. They were the dinosaurs. Like crocodiles, these prehistoric reptiles had scaly skin and laid eggs. Unlike crocodiles, however, they all lived on land. Some dinosaurs were fierce meat-eaters, while others ate only plants.

No one has ever seen a live dinosaur because they became extinct (died out) 64 million years ago. However, their bones, teeth, footprints, and even skin impressions have been preserved in rock as fossils. We can study the dinosaurs' fossil remains and can build up a picture of these strange animals that ruled our world for more than 150 million years.

EUDIMORPHODON
Not a dinosaur at all but a flying reptile, a pterosaur.

SAURORNITHOIDES
A large-eyed, large-brained meat-eater.

ARCHAEOPTERYX
As far as we know, the first bird, but with some body parts similar to the dinosaurs.

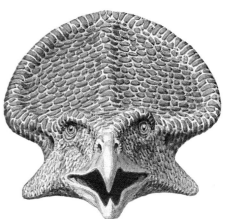

PROTOCERATOPS
An early horned dinosaur from Mongolia.

EDMONTOSAURUS
A hadrosaur, or duck-billed dinosaur, from North America.

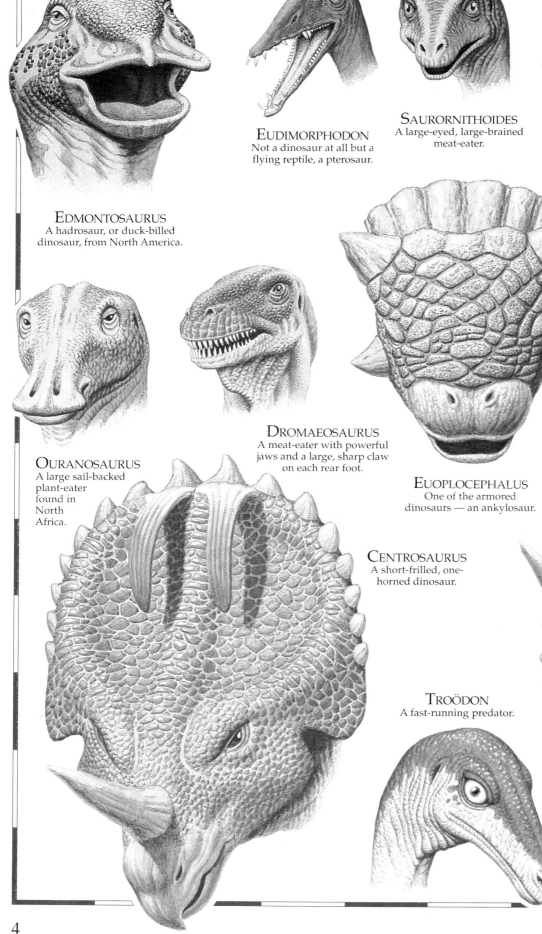

OURANOSAURUS
A large sail-backed plant-eater found in North Africa.

DROMAEOSAURUS
A meat-eater with powerful jaws and a large, sharp claw on each rear foot.

EUOPLOCEPHALUS
One of the armored dinosaurs — an ankylosaur.

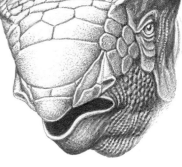

STEGOSAURUS
A plated dinosaur with an unusual method of temperature control.

ANKYLOSAURUS
The largest and last of the armored dinosaurs.

CENTROSAURUS
A short-frilled, one-horned dinosaur.

TROÖDON
A fast-running predator.

TRICERATOPS
A three-horned plant-eater.

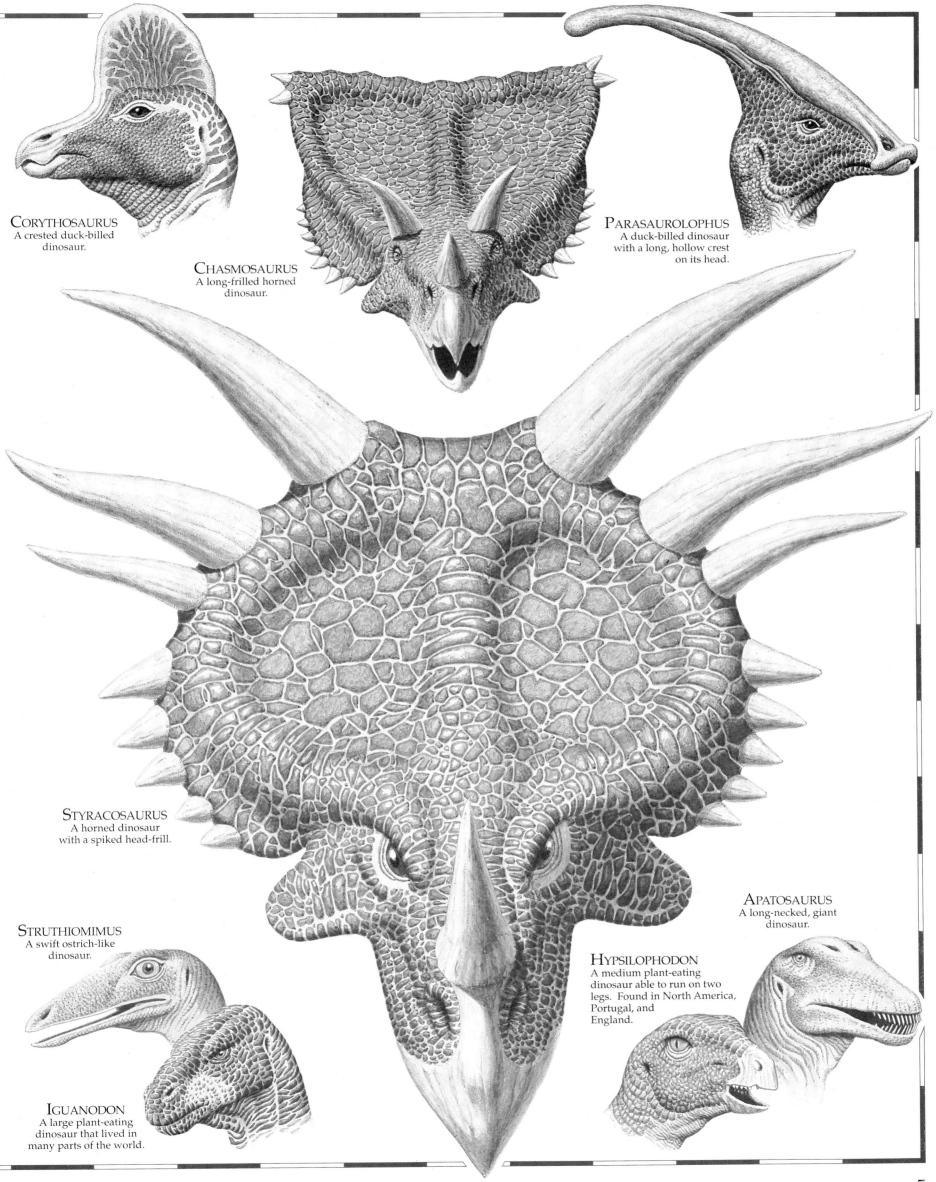

CORYTHOSAURUS
A crested duck-billed dinosaur.

CHASMOSAURUS
A long-frilled horned dinosaur.

PARASAUROLOPHUS
A duck-billed dinosaur with a long, hollow crest on its head.

STYRACOSAURUS
A horned dinosaur with a spiked head-frill.

STRUTHIOMIMUS
A swift ostrich-like dinosaur.

APATOSAURUS
A long-necked, giant dinosaur.

HYPSILOPHODON
A medium plant-eating dinosaur able to run on two legs. Found in North America, Portugal, and England.

IGUANODON
A large plant-eating dinosaur that lived in many parts of the world.

5

AGE OF THE DINOSAURS

DINOSAURS HAVE BEEN DISCOVERED all over the world. This map shows only a few of the sites that have provided literally thousands of bones. The dinosaurs shown here did not all live at the same time. They span the entire 150-million-year period that the dinosaurs ruled the Earth, from the oldest known dinosaurs *Staurikosaurus* and *Herrerasaurus* in South America to two of the last, *Tarbosaurus* and *Velociraptor,* in Asia. Dinosaur remains are found in rocks that were deposited as mud or sand when the dinosaurs were

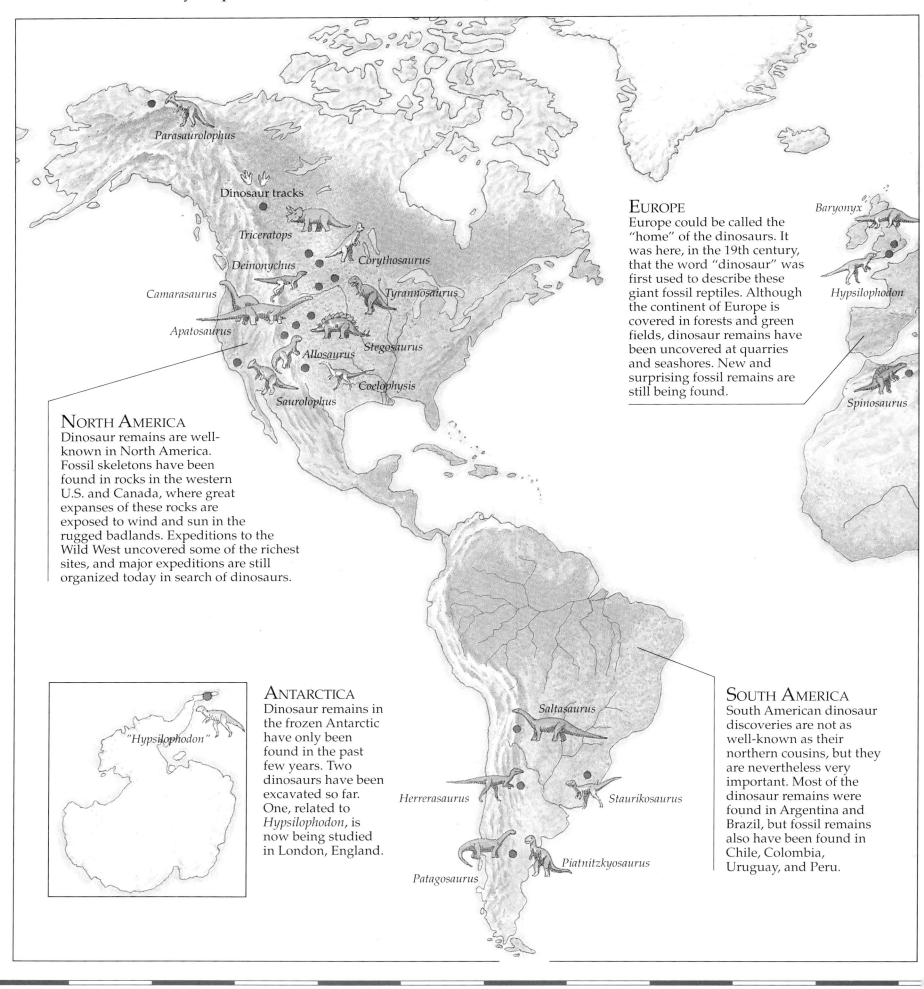

EUROPE
Europe could be called the "home" of the dinosaurs. It was here, in the 19th century, that the word "dinosaur" was first used to describe these giant fossil reptiles. Although the continent of Europe is covered in forests and green fields, dinosaur remains have been uncovered at quarries and seashores. New and surprising fossil remains are still being found.

NORTH AMERICA
Dinosaur remains are well-known in North America. Fossil skeletons have been found in rocks in the western U.S. and Canada, where great expanses of these rocks are exposed to wind and sun in the rugged badlands. Expeditions to the Wild West uncovered some of the richest sites, and major expeditions are still organized today in search of dinosaurs.

ANTARCTICA
Dinosaur remains in the frozen Antarctic have only been found in the past few years. Two dinosaurs have been excavated so far. One, related to *Hypsilophodon*, is now being studied in London, England.

SOUTH AMERICA
South American dinosaur discoveries are not as well-known as their northern cousins, but they are nevertheless very important. Most of the dinosaur remains were found in Argentina and Brazil, but fossil remains also have been found in Chile, Colombia, Uruguay, and Peru.

alive. There may be sites in other areas of the world, like Antarctica or parts of Africa, that may never be excavated because they are difficult to reach. However, dinosaur skeletons have been found in every continent, in Central America, Japan, the U.S.S.R., and in many other countries. Some have been found by accident and others as a result of major expeditions. These dinosaur remains are still being studied, and scientists continue to revise their views as new evidence is discovered. Even the names of particular dinosaurs may change as fossil remains are re-identified. Museums around the world have displays of dinosaur skeletons and skulls to help us understand what these animals looked like and how they lived. Fossils are a record of the Earth, and every new fossil found may help to fill in our picture of the world of the dinosaurs.

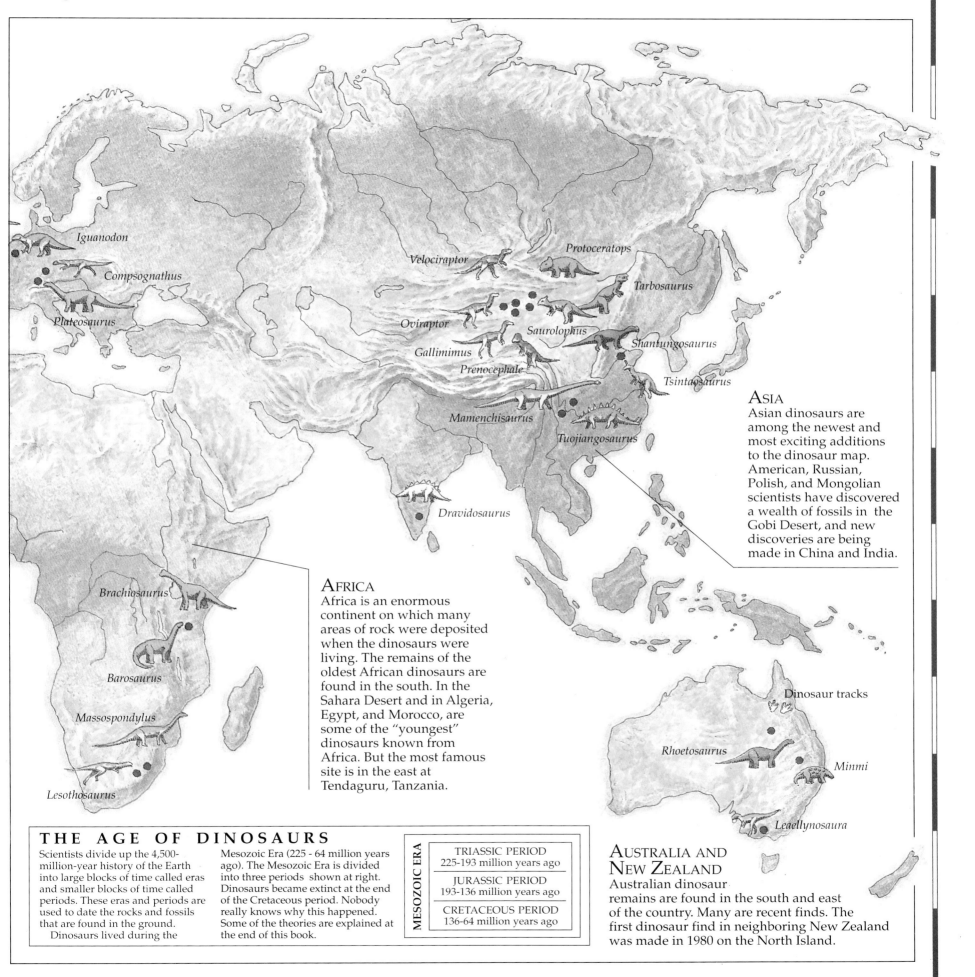

ASIA
Asian dinosaurs are among the newest and most exciting additions to the dinosaur map. American, Russian, Polish, and Mongolian scientists have discovered a wealth of fossils in the Gobi Desert, and new discoveries are being made in China and India.

AFRICA
Africa is an enormous continent on which many areas of rock were deposited when the dinosaurs were living. The remains of the oldest African dinosaurs are found in the south. In the Sahara Desert and in Algeria, Egypt, and Morocco, are some of the "youngest" dinosaurs known from Africa. But the most famous site is in the east at Tendaguru, Tanzania.

AUSTRALIA AND NEW ZEALAND
Australian dinosaur remains are found in the south and east of the country. Many are recent finds. The first dinosaur find in neighboring New Zealand was made in 1980 on the North Island.

THE AGE OF DINOSAURS
Scientists divide up the 4,500-million-year history of the Earth into large blocks of time called eras and smaller blocks of time called periods. These eras and periods are used to date the rocks and fossils that are found in the ground.

Dinosaurs lived during the Mesozoic Era (225 - 64 million years ago). The Mesozoic Era is divided into three periods shown at right. Dinosaurs became extinct at the end of the Cretaceous period. Nobody really knows why this happened. Some of the theories are explained at the end of this book.

MESOZOIC ERA	
TRIASSIC PERIOD 225-193 million years ago	
JURASSIC PERIOD 193-136 million years ago	
CRETACEOUS PERIOD 136-64 million years ago	

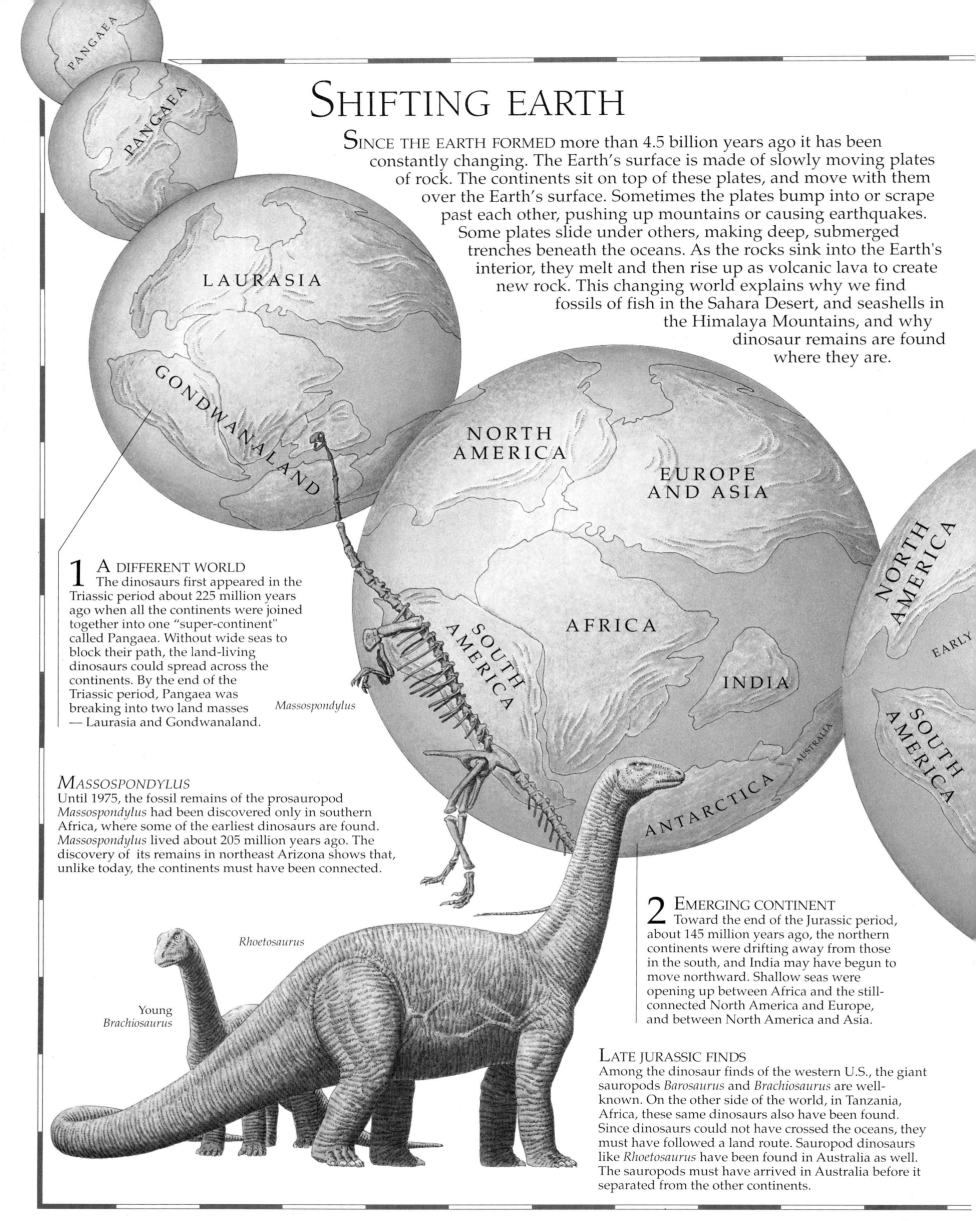

SHIFTING EARTH

SINCE THE EARTH FORMED more than 4.5 billion years ago it has been constantly changing. The Earth's surface is made of slowly moving plates of rock. The continents sit on top of these plates, and move with them over the Earth's surface. Sometimes the plates bump into or scrape past each other, pushing up mountains or causing earthquakes. Some plates slide under others, making deep, submerged trenches beneath the oceans. As the rocks sink into the Earth's interior, they melt and then rise up as volcanic lava to create new rock. This changing world explains why we find fossils of fish in the Sahara Desert, and seashells in the Himalaya Mountains, and why dinosaur remains are found where they are.

PANGAEA

PANGAEA

LAURASIA

GONDWANALAND

NORTH AMERICA

EUROPE AND ASIA

AFRICA

SOUTH AMERICA

INDIA

ANTARCTICA

AUSTRALIA

NORTH AMERICA

EARLY

SOUTH AMERICA

1 A DIFFERENT WORLD
The dinosaurs first appeared in the Triassic period about 225 million years ago when all the continents were joined together into one "super-continent" called Pangaea. Without wide seas to block their path, the land-living dinosaurs could spread across the continents. By the end of the Triassic period, Pangaea was breaking into two land masses — Laurasia and Gondwanaland.

Massospondylus

MASSOSPONDYLUS
Until 1975, the fossil remains of the prosauropod *Massospondylus* had been discovered only in southern Africa, where some of the earliest dinosaurs are found. *Massospondylus* lived about 205 million years ago. The discovery of its remains in northeast Arizona shows that, unlike today, the continents must have been connected.

Rhoetosaurus

Young *Brachiosaurus*

2 EMERGING CONTINENT
Toward the end of the Jurassic period, about 145 million years ago, the northern continents were drifting away from those in the south, and India may have begun to move northward. Shallow seas were opening up between Africa and the still-connected North America and Europe, and between North America and Asia.

LATE JURASSIC FINDS
Among the dinosaur finds of the western U.S., the giant sauropods *Barosaurus* and *Brachiosaurus* are well-known. On the other side of the world, in Tanzania, Africa, these same dinosaurs also have been found. Since dinosaurs could not have crossed the oceans, they must have followed a land route. Sauropod dinosaurs like *Rhoetosaurus* have been found in Australia as well. The sauropods must have arrived in Australia before it separated from the other continents.

Iguanodon

IGUANODON

Iguanodon, which lived about 125-110 million years ago, provides more evidence for a changing world. Its remains are well-known from north Africa, Belgium, Germany, and England. Recently, a specimen of *Iguanodon* has been found in South Dakota. Although the Atlantic Ocean had begun to divide Europe from North America at the time, the two continents were probably still joined in the north.

5 FOREVER CHANGING

Since the end of the dinosaur age, 64 million years ago, the continents have moved into their present positions. India has "collided" with Asia to form the Himalayas, and the sea has disappeared from the Sahara Desert. The existence of earthquakes and volcanoes, however, tells us that the world is still changing.

EUROPE

NORTH AMERICA

AFRICA

SOUTH AMERICA

ATLANTIC OCEAN

EASTERN ASIA

ANTARCTICA

WESTERN NORTH AMERICA

EASTERN NORTH AMERICA

SHALLOW SEA

WESTERN EUROPE AND ASIA

SHALLOW SEA

SHALLOW SEA

EARLY ATLANTIC OCEAN

AFRICA

INDIA

AUSTRALIA

ANTARCTICA

EUROPE AND ASIA

ATLANTIC OCEAN

AFRICA

EARLY ATLANTIC OCEAN

INDIA

AUSTRALIA

ANTARCTICA

3 EARLY GAPS

In the early part of the Cretaceous period the gaps between the continents were widening. The seas that came between them did not always last for long, but the Atlantic Ocean had begun to widen from the south. Antarctica and Australia were now moving away from South America and Africa.

4 SEAS

At the end of the Cretaceous period, about 80 million years ago, the Atlantic Ocean slowly spread northward as the continents continued their journeys apart. Shallow seas invaded North America, Africa, and eastern Europe, creating temporary barriers to the spread of dinosaurs from east to west across these continents.

Euoplocephalus

EAST AND WEST

Ankylosaur dinosaurs like *Pinacosaurus* and *Euoplocephalus* that lived in the late Cretaceous period are found only in eastern Asia and western North America. Two of the fiercest late Cretaceous dinosaurs—*Tyrannosaurus* and *Tarbosaurus* which are also only found in eastern Asia and western North America—are so similar that scientists believe they are the same dinosaur! The similarities between these and other dinosaurs suggest that in the late Cretaceous period dinosaurs could cross from eastern Asia to western North America by a land "bridge," but could not move into other parts of the world because of the spreading seas.

Pinacosaurus

JURASSIC SCENE

THE GREEN RIVER TODAY cuts a deep canyon through the rocks of northeastern Utah. Above the river, steeply tilted on a 215-ft. rock face, the skeletons of many dinosaurs are being uncovered, bone by bone. Since the first bone was found at Dinosaur National Monument, more than 5,000 have been discovered. The dinosaurs' remains lie where they gathered about 150 million years ago, on the bend of a wide, shallow river. In wet seasons, both the carcasses and skeletons of dinosaurs were washed into the river. Year after year their remains piled up on sandbars in the river bend. The scene below is typical of the late Jurassic period.

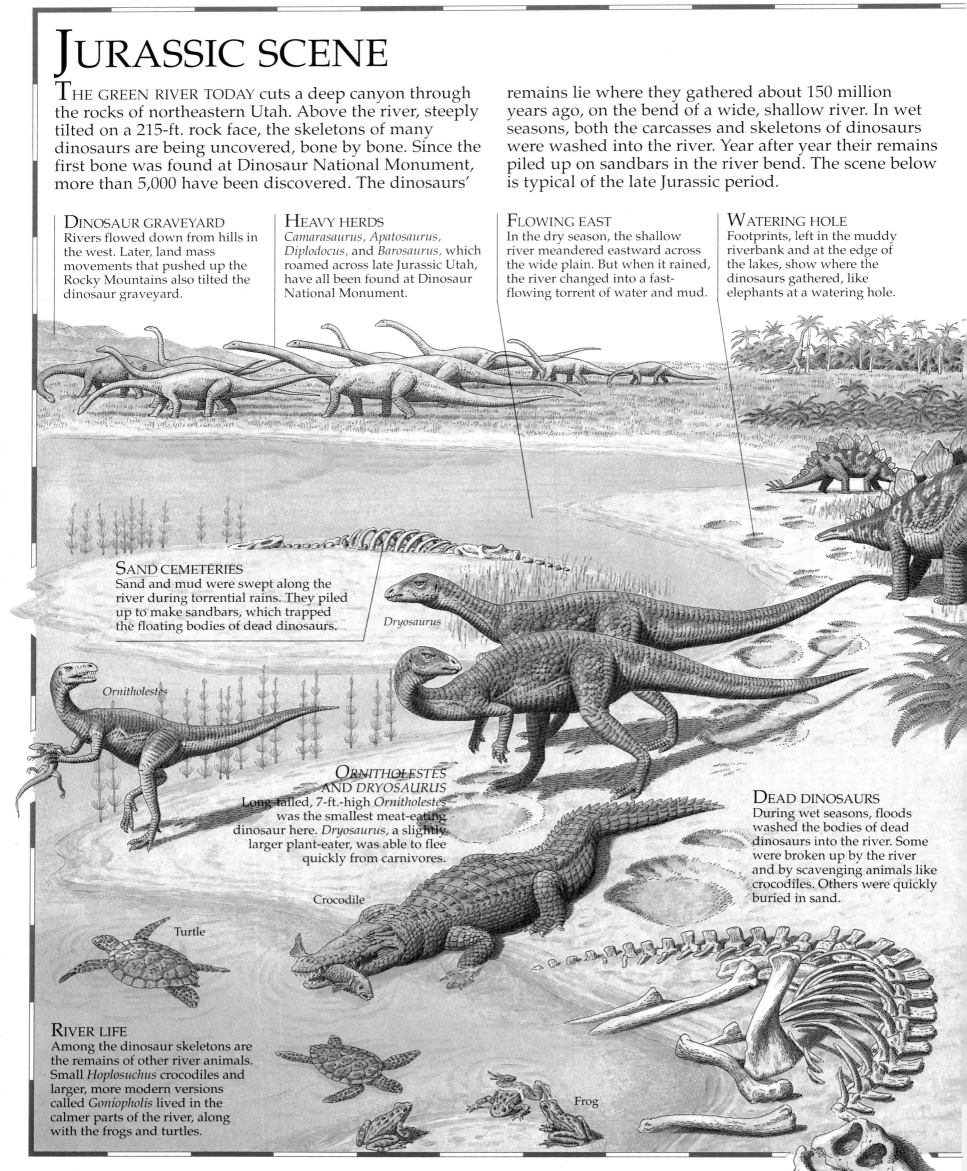

DINOSAUR GRAVEYARD
Rivers flowed down from hills in the west. Later, land mass movements that pushed up the Rocky Mountains also tilted the dinosaur graveyard.

HEAVY HERDS
Camarasaurus, Apatosaurus, Diplodocus, and *Barosaurus,* which roamed across late Jurassic Utah, have all been found at Dinosaur National Monument.

FLOWING EAST
In the dry season, the shallow river meandered eastward across the wide plain. But when it rained, the river changed into a fast-flowing torrent of water and mud.

WATERING HOLE
Footprints, left in the muddy riverbank and at the edge of the lakes, show where the dinosaurs gathered, like elephants at a watering hole.

SAND CEMETERIES
Sand and mud were swept along the river during torrential rains. They piled up to make sandbars, which trapped the floating bodies of dead dinosaurs.

Dryosaurus

Ornitholestes

ORNITHOLESTES AND *DRYOSAURUS*
Long-tailed, 7-ft.-high *Ornitholestes* was the smallest meat-eating dinosaur here. *Dryosaurus,* a slightly larger plant-eater, was able to flee quickly from carnivores.

DEAD DINOSAURS
During wet seasons, floods washed the bodies of dead dinosaurs into the river. Some were broken up by the river and by scavenging animals like crocodiles. Others were quickly buried in sand.

Crocodile

Turtle

RIVER LIFE
Among the dinosaur skeletons are the remains of other river animals. Small *Hoplosuchus* crocodiles and larger, more modern versions called *Goniopholis* lived in the calmer parts of the river, along with the frogs and turtles.

Frog

GOURMET GINKGOES

Fan-leaved ginkgo trees, typical of the period, grew in forests across the flat land, while tall conifers spread into hilly areas. Tree ferns, their leaves perched high on top of thin trunks, and benettitaleans, which looked rather like pineapples, provided food for browsing plant-eaters.

DANGEROUS CARNIVORE

Half the size of *Allosaurus*, the horned carnivore *Ceratosaurus* is not very common at Dinosaur National Monument, but it was nevertheless a dangerous predator.

SNOUT-FED

Camptosaurus, an earlier and distant relative of *Iguanodon*, had a long snout and small beak that enabled it to browse through the lower leaves of trees.

STEGOSAURUS

Walking on all fours, *Stegosaurus* used its beak to feed on plants close to the ground. With its distinctive back plates, *Stegosaurus* must have been easily recognized by other dinosaurs out on the flood plain. Of all the dinosaur remains found at Dinosaur National Monument, the bones of *Stegosaurus* are the most common.

ALLOSAURUS

The dinosaurs found at this scene had one common enemy: the terrible *Allosaurus*. One hundred and fifty million years ago, it was the largest and most abundant meat-eater living on this plain. Even the huge, lumbering sauropods were not safe. Among the 33-ft.-long adult *Allosaurus* remains, there are also young animals only 3.5 ft. tall. Young and old ended up buried in the rocks of Dinosaur National Monument.

CRETACEOUS SCENE

WHEN THE SUN ROSE on southern England about 120 million years ago, it shone on a land of open plains and hills crossed and dotted with streams and lakes. Where London is now there were mountains, and rivers flowing south through forests of monkey-puzzle evergreens and giant, fern-like cycad trees. Carpets of ferns spread out to the south, where flood plains, swamped with mud and sand from storm-filled rivers, spread across into what are today France and Belgium. Marsh ferns and horsetails thrived on the damp plains, and insects fed among the rotting vegetation. Through this scene the dinosaurs made their way, stopping to get warm in the sun. This was the world of plant-eaters such as *Iguanodon* and the fishing dinosaur *Baryonyx*.

FISHING DINOSAUR
Watching for tell-tale ripples and bubbles, *Baryonyx* dipped its claws in the river, ready to hook a passing fish.

PLATES AND SPINES
Polacanthus and *Hylaeosaurus* were rare armored dinosaurs. Protected by their bony plates and protruding spines, they browsed among low-growing ferns.

Hylaeosaurus

Polacanthus

Baryonyx

Crocodile

Lepidotes

Cricket

Dragonfly

Hard-shelled beetle

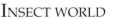
Cockroach

INSECT WORLD
Dragonflies and lacewings, little different from those living today, flitted over the dense fern growth, settling now and then on a frond. Below, hard-shelled beetles and cockroaches marched through the matted undergrowth, and noisy crickets jumped to avoid being crushed beneath a dinosaur's foot.

IN THE RIVER
Rivers, sometimes swollen by mud and rain streaming down from the mountains, were patrolled by crocodiles. Turtles occasionally left the water to bask on the river banks and watch the 3-ft.-long fish *Lepidotes* swim by. All would have feasted on any dinosaur carcass that floated by.

TROTTING
Out on the mud plain near the sea, where the creeks ran at low tide, a herd of *Hypsilophodon* would hurry toward drier land. Trotting on long-toed rear feet, and stopping to nip at young ferns, they would keep a lookout for danger.

LUMBERING SAUROPODS
In the distance, crossing from one sand bank to another, a small herd of sauropod dinosaurs might lumber toward a tree-lined bay. On the way these giants, heads high, browsed on the highest leaves of the tall tree ferns.

SOLAR SPINES
Impatiently awaiting the chance to pounce on slow or sickly prey, the spinosaur *Altispinax* might slowly move closer to the nearest dinosaur group. Along its back a sail of skin, supported on spines, would gather the sun's heat.

Sauropod

Altispinax

Hypsilophodon

Iguanodon

Turtle

IGUANODON
Iguanodon would strip the leaves from the hanging branches of conifers and tall cycads. Smaller than its cousins from the southern end of the flood plain, the 30-ft.-tall *Iguanodon* spent its time among the Cretaceous forests and plains of southern England.

DIGGING UP DINOSAURS

WHEN MOST ANIMALS DIE, their remains are broken up and destroyed by the weather and by other animals. Sometimes, however, their bodies are washed into a river or lake and quickly covered in sand and mud. In a desert the remains might be covered by wind-blown sands. This is how some dinosaurs became preserved. Over millions of years more and more sand and mud were piled on top of the remains. The sediments gradually turned into sandstone, limestone, and shale; the soft parts of the dinosaurs' bodies rotted away; and the hard and tough bones and teeth became fossils. Sometimes the dinosaurs' scaly skin lasted long enough to leave its impression in the fine mud, and fragile eggshells were also turned into fossils. Some of the bones may have been crushed. Others are preserved because their mineral component is very stable under most conditions of burial.

1 FOSSILS
Scientists have made maps showing where different kinds and different ages of rocks are found. Dinosaur fossils are found in rocks about 210-64 million years old in various parts of the world. But dinosaur discoveries are very rare. Often they lie buried in layers of rock until they are exposed on a hillside, in a quarry, or perhaps on a rocky beach. Only then can a team of experts go to work to excavate the fossil dinosaur.

DIGGING AND BRUSHING
Exposed pieces of fossil bone are traced back into the rock by carefully chiseling and brushing away the covering rock. As each bone is uncovered, the workers may need to glue broken pieces in place. The rock dust may need to be sieved to find smaller fragments of fossil.

TOOLS
Pick-axes and shovels are used to clear away large amounts of rock. Hammers and sharp chisels are needed to work close to the bone without damaging it, and brushes are used to to sweep away the dust. Protective goggles are worn to keep the digger's eyes safe, and hard-hats are essential near cliffs.

PROTECTION
Wet tissue paper is spread over the fossil to protect the surface. Thick bandages or sacking are then soaked in plaster and spread over the paper. When this has hardened, the fossil is carefully turned over, and its other side is also covered in paper and plaster bandages. When the plaster has hardened, the fossil, wearing its hard "jacket," can be lifted out.

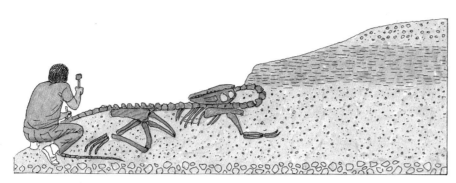

2 FIRST SIGNS

The first sign of a fossil skeleton may be only a few small pieces of broken bone sticking out of rock. The first bone that is found might be the end of the dinosaur's tail, and the rest of its skeleton may be buried deep in the rock. The rock covering the fossil remains has to be removed slowly and carefully. It may not be possible to uncover every bone, and some may need to be collected while still enclosed in rock.

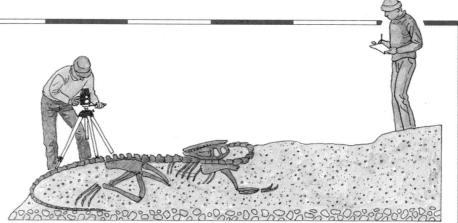

3 RECORDING DETAILS

During the excavations, maps and diagrams are drawn to show the position of each bone. Photographs may be taken to make a record of how a bone was found before it is wrapped in plaster and removed. This is important in helping the scientists identify what the bones are and where they belong in the dinosaur's skeleton. They may also help to explain how the dinosaur died, and how it became a fossil.

KEEPING COUNT

All the fossil pieces that are found must be carefully labeled. On a large excavation, it is very easy to overlook some parts if a checklist has not been made. The numbered bones are plotted on a map of the site to help scientists reassemble the skeleton. The bones may be packed in crates to await more detailed work from the laboratory.

WORK IN THE LABORATORY

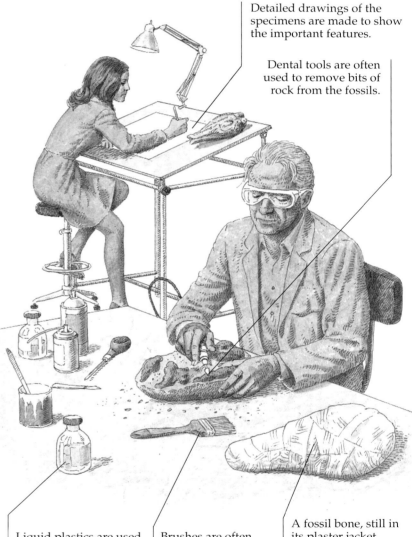

Detailed drawings of the specimens are made to show the important features.

Dental tools are often used to remove bits of rock from the fossils.

Liquid plastics are used to strengthen fossils.

Brushes are often used to clean fossils.

A fossil bone, still in its plaster jacket, waiting to be opened.

Work done in the field is quite rough. The details of the fossil bones and teeth need to be uncovered in the laboratory. Here scientists spend years carefully picking and chiseling away at the rock that is still stuck to the fossil. Microscopes are used to see the smallest details. Dentist's tools and engraving pens are often used on hard rocks, and sometimes acids are used to dissolve bits of rock. This is often dangerous, and needs to be done in special laboratories. Eventually the fragments of fossil are strengthened with liquid plastics and glued together.

LONGEST, TALLEST, HEAVIEST

THE SAUROPOD DINOSAURS were the longest, tallest, and heaviest of all the dinosaurs. They are the largest land animals ever known. The only animal that is bigger than them is the blue whale, which grows to more than 100 ft. and weighs 225 tons. One of the latest sauropod discoveries may, however, have been even longer. The sauropods were all plant-eating dinosaurs. They lived in most parts of the dinosaur world, and lasted from early Jurassic times — about 185 million years ago — until the end of the dinosaur age. Most of them, however, have been found in rocks around 145 million years old. At 60 ft. long, *Camarasaurus* was small compared to the 100-ft.-long *Ultrasaurus*. Bones of *Camarasaurus* were first discovered in Colorado in 1877, and an almost complete skeleton of a young *Camarasaurus* was later discovered at Dinosaur National Monument in Utah.

Camarasaurus

Skull

Jaw

NECK
Camarasaurus had neck vertebrae as long as 2 ft. Muscles and ligaments, like cables supporting a bridge, ran from bone to bone, and long ribs overlapped the bones behind.

COMPARING TWO SKULLS
Although both *Diplodocus* and *Camarasaurus* were large sauropods, their skulls were different shapes. The skull of *Diplodocus* was lower and flatter, with the teeth at the front of the mouth.

DIPLODOCUS SKULL
The large eye sockets are near the back of the skull. The nostrils are high up on top of the head.

SHARP SMELLER
Few smells would have escaped *Camarasaurus*, who had huge nostril cavities near the front of its skull.

PREDATOR WATCH
Like *Diplodocus*, *Camarasaurus* also had large eye sockets in the sides of the skull. However, the eyes inside the sockets were not particularly large.

Camarasaurus teeth

BLUNT TEETH
The difference between plant-eating sauropods like *Camarasaurus* and meat-eaters like *Megalosaurus* was enormous. The sharply pointed and serrated *Megalosaurus* teeth were like steak knives, but the teeth of *Camarasaurus* were thick and blunt.

Megalosaurus tooth

Diplodocus skull

DINOSAUR DIET
Diplodocus had thin, peglike teeth at the front of its mouth. It may have used these like a comb to pull leaves off twigs.

TEETH
Camarasaurus had sharp, snipping teeth all the way around its jaws.

Camarasaurus skull

ENORMOUS
Although *Camarasaurus* was one of the smaller sauropods, its size was still massive when compared with a modern human.

HEAD MUSCLES
Large open spaces between the skull bones left room for the muscles of the head to bulge. This must have lightened the weight of the skull, which the long neck had to support.

MUSCLE
Rough patches of bone show where the muscles were attached in the skull.

Camarasaurus

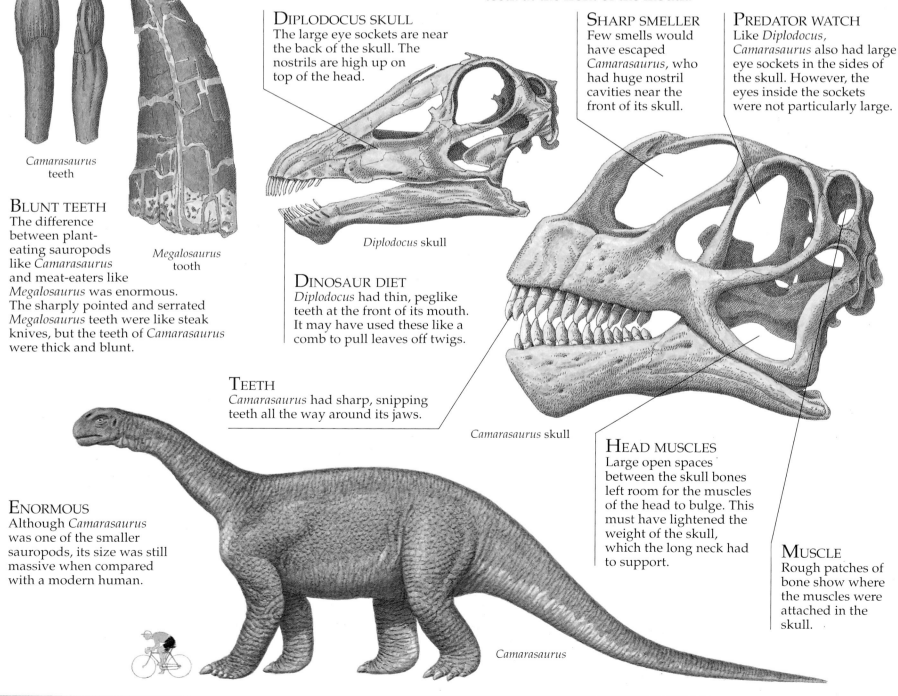

LONG NECK

Camarasaurus had a rather short neck for a sauropod, with 12 neck vertebrae in all. *Mamenchisaurus*, with 19 vertebrae, stretched its neck much longer. In fact, *Mamenchisaurus* had a neck that was about two-thirds the total length of *Camarasaurus*.

Mamenchisaurus

Neck vertebra

BARREL BODY

Ribs that were 6.5 ft. long and as thick as an arm made a huge frame around the dinosaur's heart, lungs, stomach, and other internal organs. Attached at the top to the backbone, and joined together by sheets of muscle, the ribs created the huge barrel-shaped body associated with a sauropod.

BIG BONES

The shoulder blades joined the front legs to the body and had to support a lot of the dinosaur's weight. In *Camarasaurus* these massive bones were as tall as a human adult. But the shoulder blades of *"Ultrasaurus,"* which lived at the same time, stood 3.5 ft. taller, reaching 9 ft.

Scapula (shoulder blade)

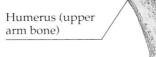

Ultrasaurus   *Camarasaurus*

Hand

Humerus (upper arm bone)

Radius (forearm)

Ulna

BIG AS A.....

Camarasaurus had hollow chambers inside its vertebrae to reduce its weight as much as possible. *Camarasaurus* means "chambered lizard" — but it still weighed more than three elephants!

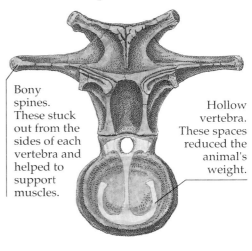

Bony spines. These stuck out from the sides of each vertebra and helped to support muscles.

Hollow vertebra. These spaces reduced the animal's weight.

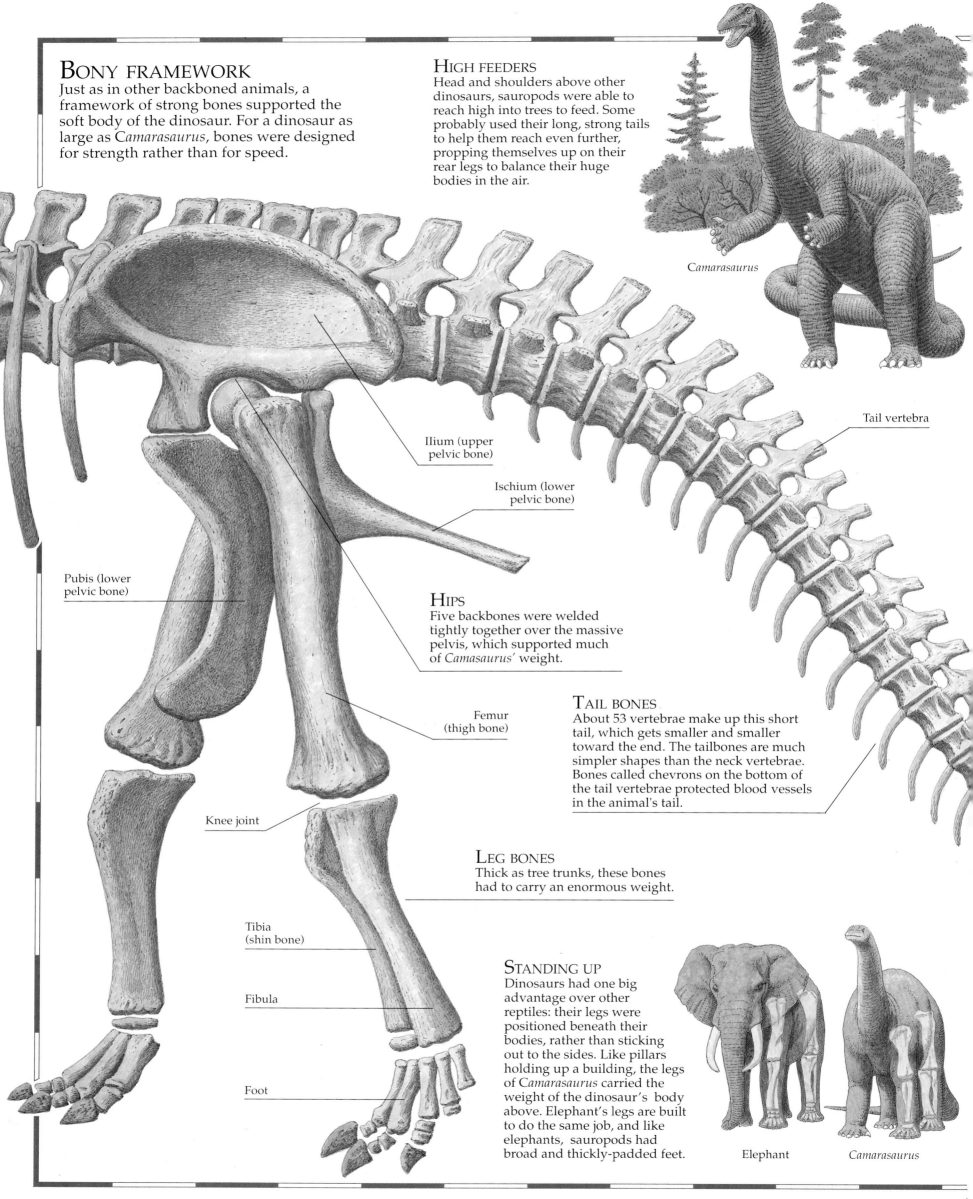

BONY FRAMEWORK

Just as in other backboned animals, a framework of strong bones supported the soft body of the dinosaur. For a dinosaur as large as *Camarasaurus*, bones were designed for strength rather than for speed.

HIGH FEEDERS

Head and shoulders above other dinosaurs, sauropods were able to reach high into trees to feed. Some probably used their long, strong tails to help them reach even further, propping themselves up on their rear legs to balance their huge bodies in the air.

Camarasaurus

Ilium (upper pelvic bone)

Ischium (lower pelvic bone)

Tail vertebra

Pubis (lower pelvic bone)

HIPS

Five backbones were welded tightly together over the massive pelvis, which supported much of *Camasaurus'* weight.

Femur (thigh bone)

TAIL BONES

About 53 vertebrae make up this short tail, which gets smaller and smaller toward the end. The tailbones are much simpler shapes than the neck vertebrae. Bones called chevrons on the bottom of the tail vertebrae protected blood vessels in the animal's tail.

Knee joint

LEG BONES

Thick as tree trunks, these bones had to carry an enormous weight.

Tibia (shin bone)

Fibula

STANDING UP

Dinosaurs had one big advantage over other reptiles: their legs were positioned beneath their bodies, rather than sticking out to the sides. Like pillars holding up a building, the legs of *Camarasaurus* carried the weight of the dinosaur's body above. Elephant's legs are built to do the same job, and like elephants, sauropods had broad and thickly-padded feet.

Foot

Elephant   *Camarasaurus*

18

DINOSAURS IN SCALE

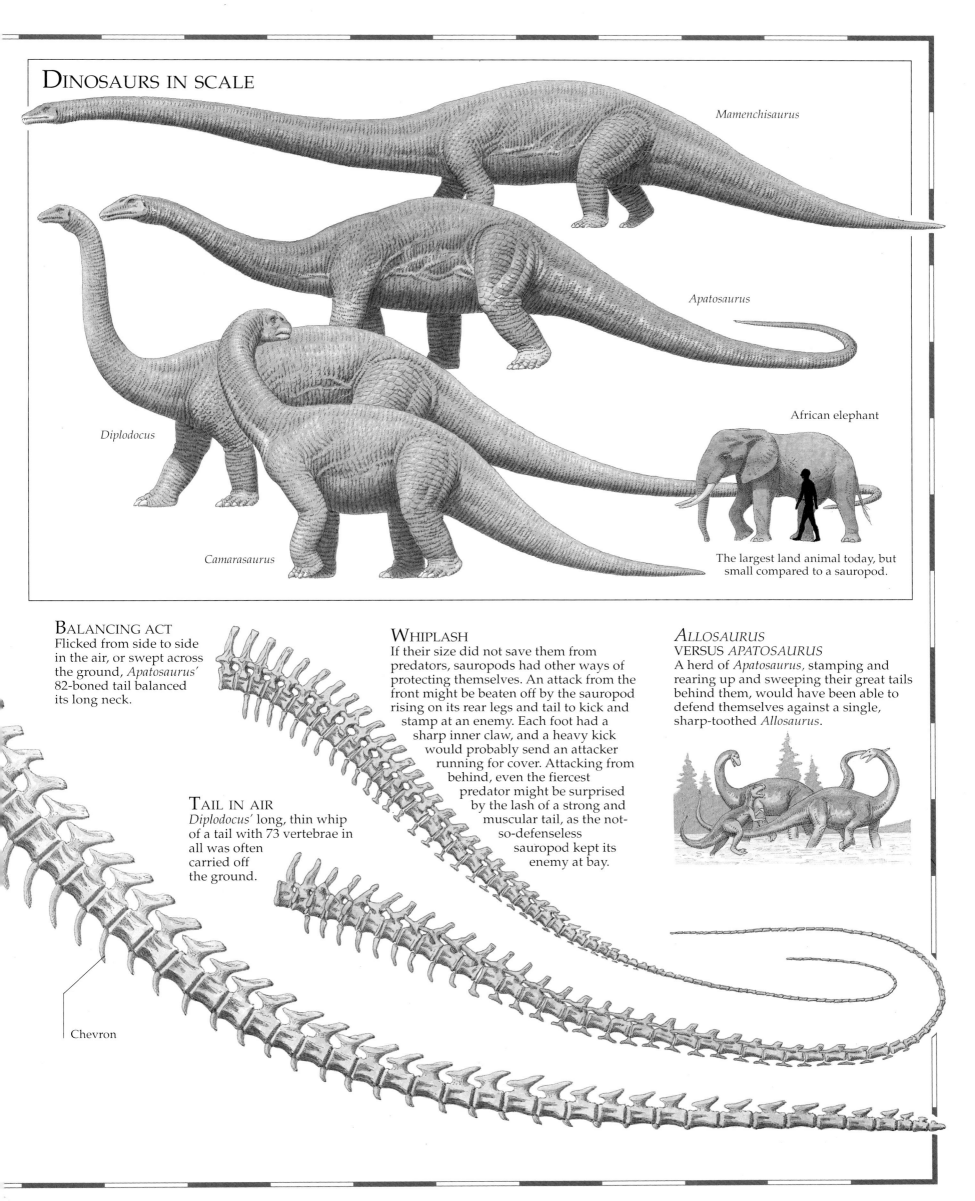

Mamenchisaurus

Apatosaurus

Diplodocus

African elephant

Camarasaurus

The largest land animal today, but small compared to a sauropod.

BALANCING ACT
Flicked from side to side in the air, or swept across the ground, *Apatosaurus'* 82-boned tail balanced its long neck.

TAIL IN AIR
Diplodocus' long, thin whip of a tail with 73 vertebrae in all was often carried off the ground.

Chevron

WHIPLASH
If their size did not save them from predators, sauropods had other ways of protecting themselves. An attack from the front might be beaten off by the sauropod rising on its rear legs and tail to kick and stamp at an enemy. Each foot had a sharp inner claw, and a heavy kick would probably send an attacker running for cover. Attacking from behind, even the fiercest predator might be surprised by the lash of a strong and muscular tail, as the not-so-defenseless sauropod kept its enemy at bay.

ALLOSAURUS VERSUS APATOSAURUS
A herd of *Apatosaurus*, stamping and rearing up and sweeping their great tails behind them, would have been able to defend themselves against a single, sharp-toothed *Allosaurus*.

MEAT-EATERS

CARNOSAURS WERE the giant killers of the dinosaur world. As active hunters, they needed muscular bodies and strong, powerful legs. Some, as tall as houses, were the largest animals ever to walk on two legs. Even carnosaurs that fed on dead animals needed strength to tear meat from the bones of their prey. Sharp teeth and claws were essential for meat-eaters, both for attacking live animals and for defending themselves. *Allosaurus* was one of the most common types of carnosaur. It lived about 150-140 million years ago. The bones of more than 60 *Allosaurus* have been found in one quarry in Utah. *Allosaurus* grew to as long as 36 ft., and may have weighed up to two tons. Because of its huge size, *Allosaurus* probably could not move quickly over long distances.

Neck vertebra

Allosaurus

HEAVY-HEADED
Allosaurus' curved neck had to be strong and flexible to carry its heavy head. Nine vertebrae made the neck short and muscular. Rough surfaces on the spine show scientists where muscles were attached.

Scapula

Humerus

Ulna

Radius

Hand

ALLOSAURUS SKULL
The huge skull had large spaces, or "windows," between the bones, which made it light but strong.

STRANGE BUMPS
Allosaurus had a rough, bony bump over each eye. This may have helped one animal recognize another by the different shape.

BIG-EYED
Allosaurus' big eye sockets mean that it probably had large eyes.

SMALL BUT USEFUL
Small but sturdy arms and hands helped *Allosaurus* grasp its prey. Its three-fingered hands had sharp claws that could tear into flesh.

Allosaurus

A REAL KILLER
More than 70 curved, saw-edged teeth lined *Allosaurus'* jaws. Pointing backward, they forced chunks of meat into its hungry, gaping mouth.

MUSCLE-BOUND
Wide-mouthed meat-eaters like *Allosaurus* had large muscles for opening and closing their jaws. These big, bulging muscles, attached to the inside of the head, could expand in the skull's "window" spaces.

LONG AND DANGEROUS
Allosaurus' skull was almost 3.5 ft. long. Hinged at the rear, the jaws could swing open, closing down in a ferocious bite.

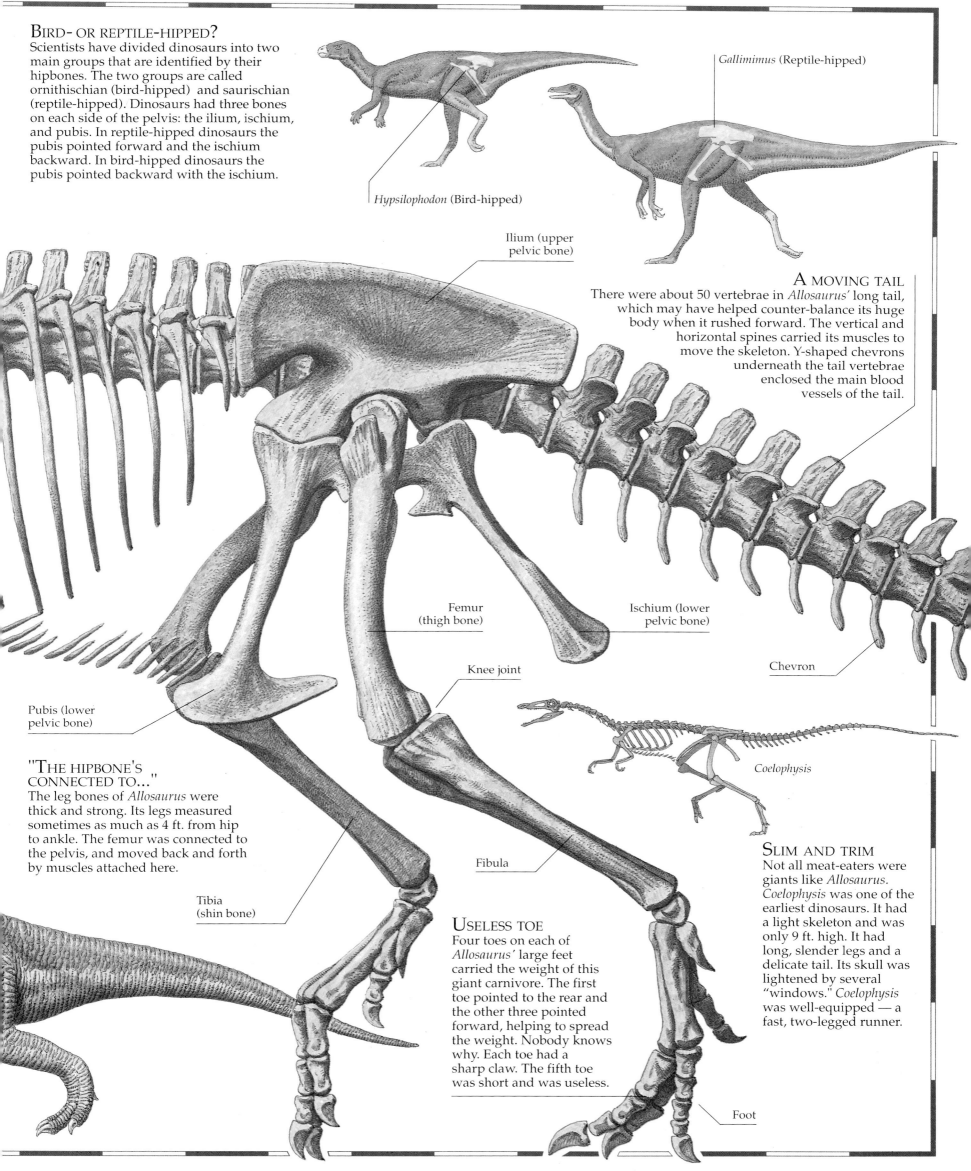

BIRD- OR REPTILE-HIPPED?
Scientists have divided dinosaurs into two main groups that are identified by their hipbones. The two groups are called ornithischian (bird-hipped) and saurischian (reptile-hipped). Dinosaurs had three bones on each side of the pelvis: the ilium, ischium, and pubis. In reptile-hipped dinosaurs the pubis pointed forward and the ischium backward. In bird-hipped dinosaurs the pubis pointed backward with the ischium.

Gallimimus (Reptile-hipped)

Hypsilophodon (Bird-hipped)

Ilium (upper pelvic bone)

A MOVING TAIL
There were about 50 vertebrae in *Allosaurus'* long tail, which may have helped counter-balance its huge body when it rushed forward. The vertical and horizontal spines carried its muscles to move the skeleton. Y-shaped chevrons underneath the tail vertebrae enclosed the main blood vessels of the tail.

Femur (thigh bone)

Ischium (lower pelvic bone)

Chevron

Pubis (lower pelvic bone)

Knee joint

Coelophysis

"THE HIPBONE'S CONNECTED TO..."
The leg bones of *Allosaurus* were thick and strong. Its legs measured sometimes as much as 4 ft. from hip to ankle. The femur was connected to the pelvis, and moved back and forth by muscles attached here.

Tibia (shin bone)

Fibula

USELESS TOE
Four toes on each of *Allosaurus'* large feet carried the weight of this giant carnivore. The first toe pointed to the rear and the other three pointed forward, helping to spread the weight. Nobody knows why. Each toe had a sharp claw. The fifth toe was short and was useless.

SLIM AND TRIM
Not all meat-eaters were giants like *Allosaurus*. *Coelophysis* was one of the earliest dinosaurs. It had a light skeleton and was only 9 ft. high. It had long, slender legs and a delicate tail. Its skull was lightened by several "windows." *Coelophysis* was well-equipped — a fast, two-legged runner.

Foot

NORTH AMERICA

FROM ALASKA in the north to Mexico in the south, from Nova Scotia in the east to California in the west, North America is a treasure-trove of dinosaur discoveries. Famous dinosaurs like *Tyrannosaurus* and *Stegosaurus* have been found only in North America, and new kinds of dinosaurs are still being found. Huge areas of dinosaur-age rock, laid bare in the semi-desert badlands of the West, have produced some of the world's richest fossil sites. The map (right) shows the major sites. In Utah, the Dinosaur National Monument displays giant dinosaur skeletons lying as they were found. Further north, in Alberta, Canada, a whole area of dinosaur finds has been made into a Provincial Park. When dinosaurs were very new to North America, they had close contact with the dinosaurs in Europe. We know that the dinosaurs that came later were more closely related to those found in Eastern Asia.

COLVILLE RIVER
Alaska

Parasaurolophus

Footprints

PEACE RIVER
British Columbia Canada

DRUMHELLER
Alberta Canada

DINOSAUR PROVINCIAL PARK
Alberta Canada

Edmontosaurus

Corythosaurus

HELL CREEK
Montana

Tyrannosaurus

CHOTEAU
Montana

Eggs and nest

COMO RIDGE
Wyoming

SOUTH OF BILLINGS
Montana

Deinonychus

Triceratops

Diplodocus

LANCE CREEK
Wyoming

CLEVELAND - LLOYD
DINOSAUR QUARRY
Utah

GARDEN PARK
Colorado

Allosaurus

Stegosaurus

DINOSAUR
NATIONAL MONUMENT
Utah/Colorado

SAN JUAN RIVER
New Mexico

GHOST RANCH
New Mexico

Saurolophus

Pentaceratops

MORENO HILLS
California

Coelophysis

Footprints

COAHUILA STATE
Mexico

PALUXY RIVER
Texas

Panoplosaurus

Deinonychus

FOOTPRINTS IN THE MUD

Dinosaurs large and small left behind more than just their bones when they died. While walking in mud or wet sand on the banks of rivers and lakes, many dinosaur feet left their mark. In fact, we can count 1,700 dinosaur footprints in the rocks of the Peace River canyon, Canada. These were made by herds of hadrosaurs and groups of meat-eaters, showing what a busy and dangerous highway this was.

Deinonychus   *Saurolophus*   *Corythosaurus*   *Parasaurolophus*

Kritosaurus

Maiasaura

QUICK-THINKING, FAST MOVING

Deinonychus is one of the dinosaurs that changed our whole view of the dinosaur world. Its fossil remains, discovered in 1964 in the badlands of Montana, show that *Deinonychus* was anything but a slow-moving reptile. Built for speed and quick attacking movements, it was an intelligent and active animal.

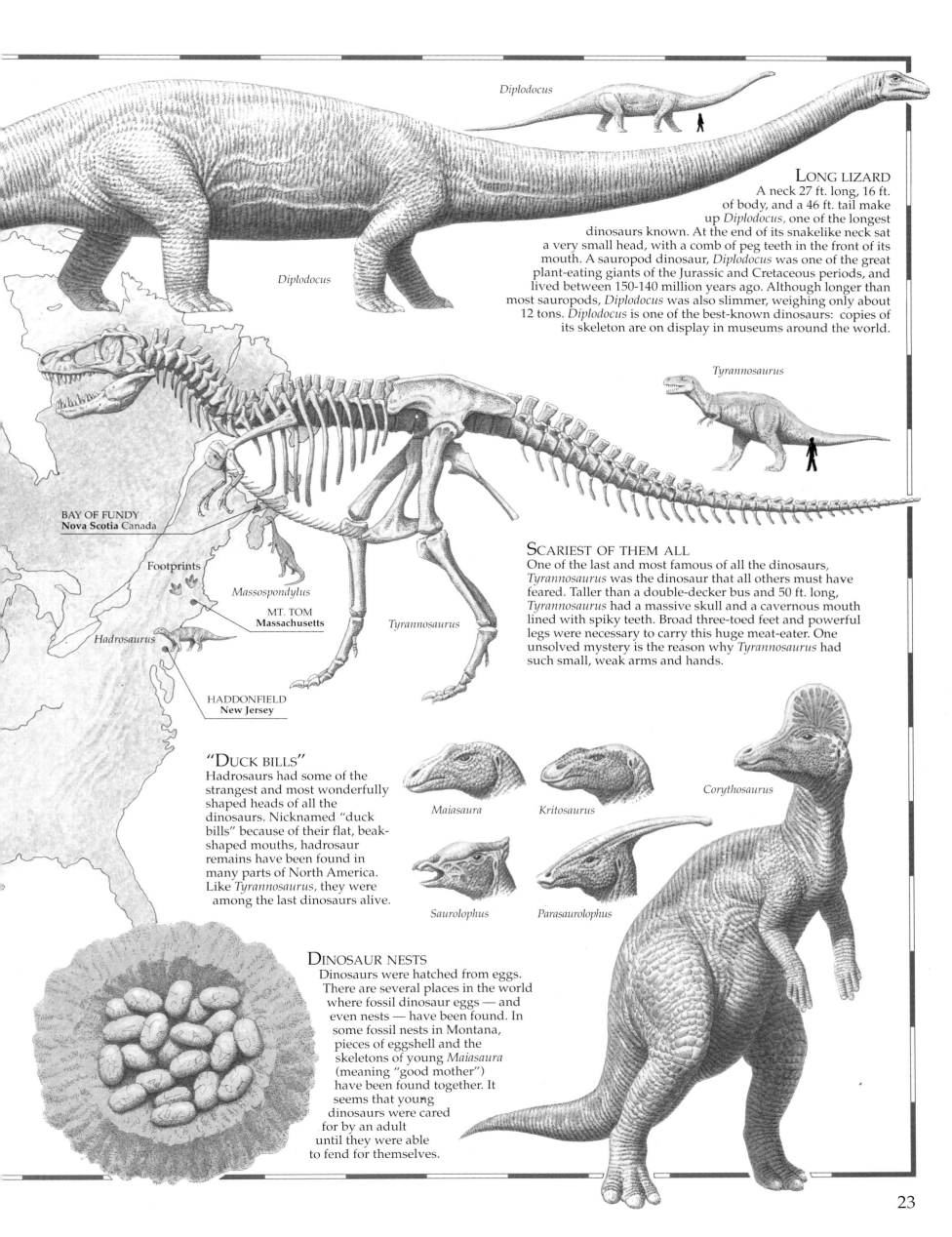

Diplodocus

LONG LIZARD

A neck 27 ft. long, 16 ft. of body, and a 46 ft. tail make up *Diplodocus,* one of the longest dinosaurs known. At the end of its snakelike neck sat a very small head, with a comb of peg teeth in the front of its mouth. A sauropod dinosaur, *Diplodocus* was one of the great plant-eating giants of the Jurassic and Cretaceous periods, and lived between 150-140 million years ago. Although longer than most sauropods, *Diplodocus* was also slimmer, weighing only about 12 tons. *Diplodocus* is one of the best-known dinosaurs: copies of its skeleton are on display in museums around the world.

Diplodocus

Tyrannosaurus

BAY OF FUNDY
Nova Scotia Canada

Footprints

Massospondylus

MT. TOM
Massachusetts

Hadrosaurus

Tyrannosaurus

HADDONFIELD
New Jersey

SCARIEST OF THEM ALL

One of the last and most famous of all the dinosaurs, *Tyrannosaurus* was the dinosaur that all others must have feared. Taller than a double-decker bus and 50 ft. long, *Tyrannosaurus* had a massive skull and a cavernous mouth lined with spiky teeth. Broad three-toed feet and powerful legs were necessary to carry this huge meat-eater. One unsolved mystery is the reason why *Tyrannosaurus* had such small, weak arms and hands.

"DUCK BILLS"

Hadrosaurs had some of the strangest and most wonderfully shaped heads of all the dinosaurs. Nicknamed "duck bills" because of their flat, beak-shaped mouths, hadrosaur remains have been found in many parts of North America. Like *Tyrannosaurus,* they were among the last dinosaurs alive.

Maiasaura

Kritosaurus

Corythosaurus

Saurolophus

Parasaurolophus

DINOSAUR NESTS

Dinosaurs were hatched from eggs. There are several places in the world where fossil dinosaur eggs — and even nests — have been found. In some fossil nests in Montana, pieces of eggshell and the skeletons of young *Maiasaura* (meaning "good mother") have been found together. It seems that young dinosaurs were cared for by an adult until they were able to fend for themselves.

23

DINOSAUR PARK

ALONG THE BANKS OF THE RED DEER RIVER in Alberta, Canada, is one of the greatest dinosaur sites in the world. Almost 350 dinosaur skeletons have been collected there, and new remains are discovered each year. This area of Alberta is considered so important for its fossils that it was made into Dinosaur Provincial Park. It is now a United Nations World Heritage Site, along with the pyramids of Egypt and the Galapagos Islands. The dinosaurs lived here about 75 million years ago, near the end of the dinosaur age when the climate was warm and the area was covered in subtropical plants. Today, rain and snow erode the rock formations found in the spectacular badlands, and uncover the rich dinosaur remains. Hadrosaurs are common among the skeletons of large dinosaurs found, and dense concentrations of the horned *Centrosaurus* have been uncovered. Armored *Euoplocephalus* and the tyrannosaurid *Albertosaurus* are among the large dinosaurs that once wandered through this dinosaur park.

Albertosaurus

A REAL TERROR
One of the most common meat-eating dinosaurs in the park, *Albertosaurus* belonged to the same family as *Tyrannosaurus*. Smaller and faster moving, this killer would have terrorized the many plant-eaters.

THE GREAT DINOSAUR RUSH

In the early 1900s, dinosaur collectors rushed to the land along the Red Deer River. The fossil treasure of hadrosaurs, ankylosaurs, and horned dinosaurs was brought out of the badlands on horse-drawn wagons or river rafts.

DINOSAUR AIRLIFT

Collecting today in Dinosaur Provincial Park still requires hard work and patience. Great blocks of dinosaur bones are lifted out of the area using helicopters and powerful trucks, and are then taken to a new museum in the province.

RED DEER RIVER
The Red Deer River flows through the rugged, deserted plains of Alberta. Along its course it cuts through the rocks formed of ancient sediments, which now produce the eroded badlands scenery.

Euoplocephalus

Lambeosaurus

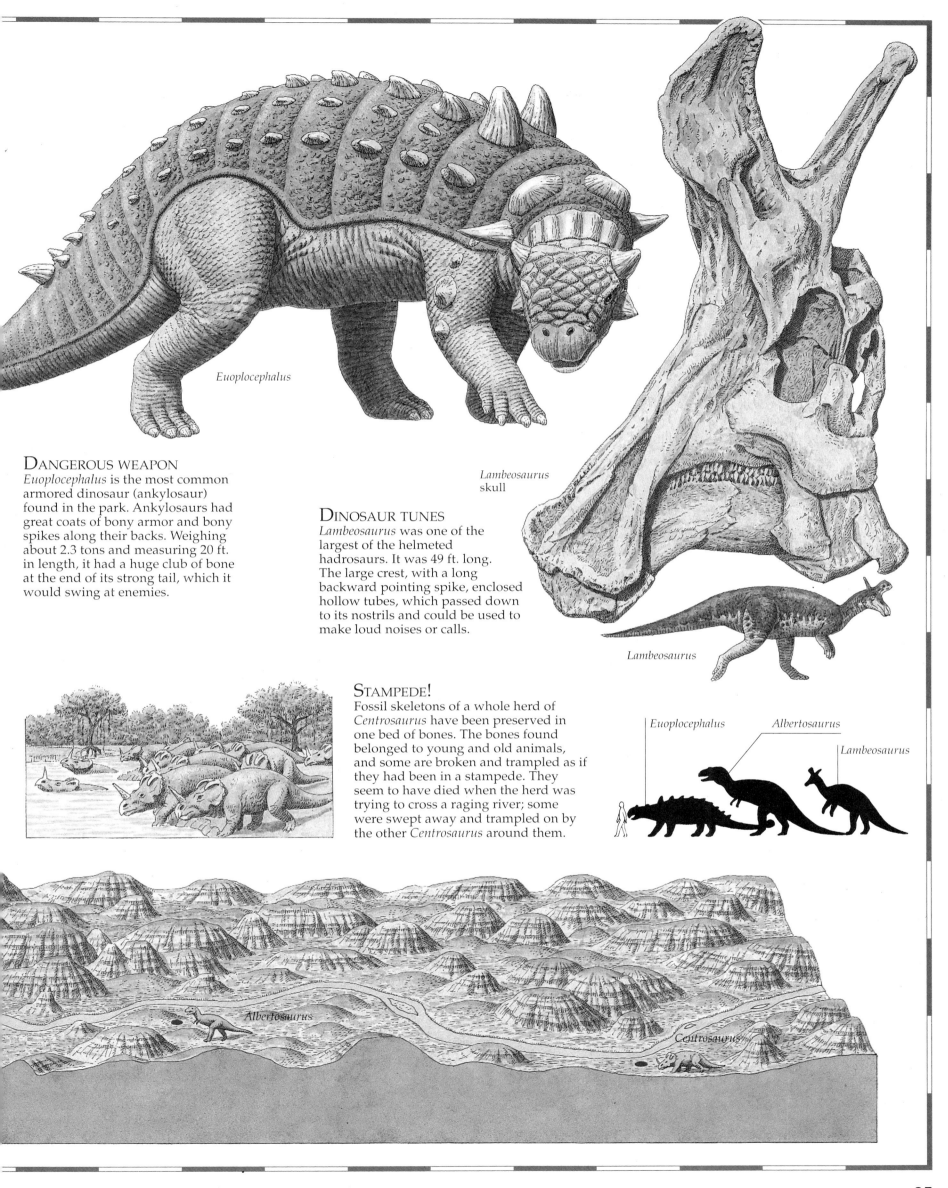

DANGEROUS WEAPON
Euoplocephalus is the most common armored dinosaur (ankylosaur) found in the park. Ankylosaurs had great coats of bony armor and bony spikes along their backs. Weighing about 2.3 tons and measuring 20 ft. in length, it had a huge club of bone at the end of its strong tail, which it would swing at enemies.

Euoplocephalus

DINOSAUR TUNES
Lambeosaurus was one of the largest of the helmeted hadrosaurs. It was 49 ft. long. The large crest, with a long backward pointing spike, enclosed hollow tubes, which passed down to its nostrils and could be used to make loud noises or calls.

Lambeosaurus
skull

Lambeosaurus

STAMPEDE!
Fossil skeletons of a whole herd of *Centrosaurus* have been preserved in one bed of bones. The bones found belonged to young and old animals, and some are broken and trampled as if they had been in a stampede. They seem to have died when the herd was trying to cross a raging river; some were swept away and trampled on by the other *Centrosaurus* around them.

Euoplocephalus   *Albertosaurus*

Lambeosaurus

Albertosaurus

Centrosaurus

HORNED FACES

TRICERATOPS IS PERHAPS THE BEST-KNOWN of the ceratopsids—the horned-face dinosaurs—that were among the last dinosaurs to appear on Earth. Armed with nose and eyebrow horns, a large skull made even larger by a bony frill extension at the rear, and a heavy bulky body, *Triceratops* looked like the rhinoceroses of the dinosaur world. Powerful limbs helped these dinosaurs stand their ground against an attacker, while protecting themselves and their young. Horned dinosaurs seem to have lived in herds, roaming open spaces and cropping plants with their toothless beaks as they went. Paleontologists have divided the horned dinosaurs into two groups: a short-frilled group that includes *Centrosaurus* and *Styracosaurus*, and a long-frilled group that includes *Torosaurus* and *Pentaceratops*. While the short-frilled dinosaurs usually have long nose horns and short eyebrow horns, the long-frilled animals have short, blunt horns on their noses and long, pointed brow horns. *Triceratops* seems to be somewhere between the two. Only the bony horn core is found as a fossil; the actual horn that covered these and made them much larger is not preserved. The horned dinosaurs have only been found in North America. It seems that they appeared too late in the changing world to spread into other continents.

TRICERATOPS
Triceratops, "three-horned face," appeared about 72 million years ago.

BIG-HEADED
Nose horns, eyebrow horns, and a frill fanning out from the rear of the skull all added to the head size of the horned dinosaurs. Extra bone grew on top of the skull between the eyes, to strengthen the whole structure.

Eyebrow horns

Nose horn

BRAIN BOX
A human skull is about 13 times shorter than *Torosaurus'* skull. However, most of the human skull is filled with the brain, unlike *Torosaurus',* which was filled with lots of muscle and bone and only a small brain.

Frill fanning

SKELETON FOR STRENGTH
The skeleton of the horned dinosaurs was specially adapted to carry their great weight. The first three neck bones behind the skull were joined together into one solid, strong bone. Eight of the vertebrae were joined to the pelvis, rather than the usual five. The horned dinosaurs walked on four sturdy legs, rather than just two rear legs.

Bony tendons

Eight vertebrae joining pelvis

Heavy frilled skull

Fused neck bones

Strong legs

Weight-spreading feet

WHAT A FRILL!

The horned dinosaurs' bony frills came in different shapes and sizes. The frills anchored huge muscles, which ran down through spaces in the skull, behind the eyebrow horns, to the jaws. The bony frills also protected the neck when the head was raised. When their heads were lowered and the frill stood high above the ground, other dinosaurs would have seen them and kept their distance. *Torosaurus'* skull was the longest of all, nearly 8.5 ft. long.

WARNING SIGNALS

Many animals living today have some form of horns. Horns like those of *Triceratops* may have been used only as a warning signal to enemies, or as weapons to defend themselves when attacked. Horns may also have been some kind of dinosaur status symbol, or mark of rank within the herd.

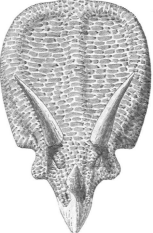

Torosaurus

FRILLED FAMILIES

Many horned dinosaurs had two large "windows" in their bony frills, which helped to make them lighter. Strangely, *Triceratops* had a solid frill with no spaces. *Triceratops* is also unusual because although it had a short frill, it also had the short nose horn and long eyebrow horns of its long-frilled relatives.

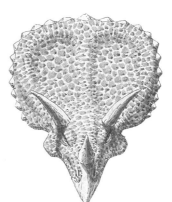

Pentaceratops

SLICE AND SHEAR

Triceratops and the other horned dinosaurs were plant-eaters. They had no teeth at the front of their mouths, but had a strong and sharp hooked beak that could cut through tough plants. Behind the beak, sharply toothed jaws sliced through leaves like a pair of garden shears.

WHAT A WEIGHT!

Triceratops weighed about 6 tons, as much as a big truck, but it was not the heaviest horned dinosaur. *Torosaurus* weighed about 9 tons. To carry these huge weights, horned dinosaurs had thick and powerful legs. The front legs also had to bear the weight of their skulls.

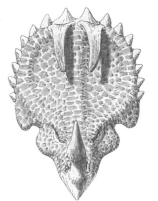

Centrosaurus

SPREAD THAT LOAD!

Large, heavy animals like elephants have broad, well-padded feet to spread the load of their weight. They may be able to move fast over short distances, but their feet are built for strength rather than speed. *Triceratops'* feet spread its weight over a wide area.

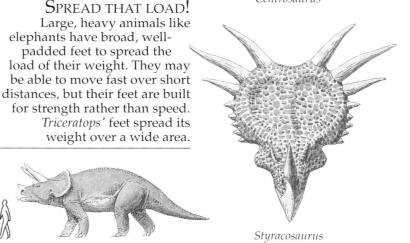

Triceratops

Styracosaurus

DINOSAUR FEASTS

DIFFERENT DINOSAURS ate different kinds of food. While plant-eaters, or herbivores, lived on leaves and shoots, meat-eaters, or carnivores, fed on other animals, including other dinosaurs. In one part of Alberta, Canada, fossil remains show that there were only four or five meat-eaters for every 100 plant-eaters. Some dinosaurs probably ate both meat and plants, as well as insects. Some carnivores were able to attack and kill their prey, moving quickly alone or in packs. Others did not kill their own prey, but fed on the remains of a carcass left behind, or perhaps on other dinosaurs that died naturally. Both hunters and scavengers needed sharp teeth and claws to rip and cut through the tough, scaly skin. Strong jaws and backward-pointing teeth forced large chunks of flesh into their mouths. There was no shortage of meals for the meat-eating dinosaurs!

DEADLY AIM
The biggest flesh-eating animal ever, *Tyrannosaurus* could charge down on its prey over short distances at a speed of 18 mph. Its strength was deadly.

COME AND GET IT!
A pack of fast *Deinonychus* could tackle dinosaurs larger than themselves. Slashing claws and a gripping bite wore down the victims, providing a meal for all.

SCAVENGER
The vertebrae of *Apatosaurus* have been found with *Allosaurus* teeth-marks. We are not sure if the giant sauropod died naturally and was found by the hungry *Allosaurus*.

CANNIBALS
Coelophysis skeletons found in New Mexico contained the skeletons of their young. These were too large to be unborn babies. It seems that *Coelophysis* ate their offspring.

Allosaurus

Dilophosaurus

Deinonychus

Coelophysis

SMALLER AND SMALLER
Fast-running, lightly built dinosaurs like *Coelophysis* were well designed to catch other, smaller dinosaurs, as well as insects and lizardlike reptiles. In one of the best discoveries of *Coelophysis*, dozens of their skeletons were found together, apparently washed down a river in a flood.

RUNNING HUNTER
Deinonychus, one of the deadliest dinosaurs, had many features of an efficient hunter. Powerful jaws lined with jagged teeth and a curved claw on both feet inflicted deadly wounds on its prey. A strong tail counter-balanced its body at high speeds, as it stalked and chased scared plant-eaters.

STRONG YET DELICATE
One of the first large meat-eaters, *Dilophosaurus* first appeared about 190 million years ago, about 40 million years before *Allosaurus*. Twenty ft. long, with strong legs and a long tail, *Dilophosaurus* had more delicate jaws than later carnosaurs, and may have been a scavenger.

Tyrannosaurus

Troödon

NEVER HUNGRY

Allosaurus was a common predator in North America 150 million years ago, during the late Jurassic period. Fossil remains of several plant-eating dinosaurs have been found with the skeletons of *Allosaurus*, including *Stegosaurus*, *Camptosaurus*, and the huge *Camarasaurus*.

THREE-FINGERED SMARTY

Troödon had a sharp sickle-shaped claw on each foot and a strong tail. A three-fingered hand enabled it to hold its victim, and a particularly large brain and large eyes made it a good hunter by day or night. For many years, all that was found of *Troödon* was one tooth.

REPTILE TYRANT

Tyrannosaurus must have been the most fearsome hunter in the entire dinosaur world. Its size, weight, and power place it at the top of the meat-eating dinosaurs, yet none of this helped when the dinosaurs became extinct. Even the tyrant of the reptiles could not survive this catastrophe.

ON THE MOVE

THE SAUROPODS WERE the largest animals ever known on land. They lived all over the world, from about 190 to 64 million years ago. Their five-toed hands and feet were made like elephants' feet and had a large, fleshy heel. Pillar-like arms and legs supported a body that was bigger than several elephants put together. All of the sauropod dinosaurs had very long necks and equally long tails. Their heads were very small compared to their bodies. As plant-eaters, they probably spent much of their time eating. The sauropods defended themselves by using their long, whiplash tails and large, stamping feet.

Apatosaurus belongs to the group of sauropods that includes *Diplodocus*, *Barosaurus*, and *Mamenchisaurus*. *Apatosaurus* was 76 ft. long, 17 ft. high at its hips, and weighed about 42 tons. For a long time scientists believed that the sauropods were so large and so heavy that they could only have lived in water, which would have helped to support their weight. However, when *Apatosaurus* footprints were found in rock in Texas, scientists changed their minds. The huge footprints had not been made in mud deep under water but in sand, damp enough to keep the print sharp. Right behind the *Apatosaurus* prints are those of a well-known land prowler — a preying *Allosaurus*.

MISTAKEN IDENTITY
Apatosaurus used to be called *Brontosaurus*. This name is no longer used because scientists have discovered that the first bones found were given the name *Apatosaurus*.

BOTTOMLESS PIT
About 150 million years ago, during the late Jurassic period, herds of *Apatosaurus* roamed across the plains of North America. *Apatosaurus* probably had to eat tons of leaves and twigs every day, constantly feeding its huge body.

ONE HEAD IS BETTER THAN TWO

No skull of *Apatosaurus* has ever been found and for nearly 100 years scientists used the skull of another sauropod, *Camarasaurus*, to complete the skeleton. It was not until 1979 that scientists agreed that *Apatosaurus* had a skull more like *Diplodocus*.

FOSSILIZED FOREVER

The fossilized footprints of animals are made when prints in soft mud or sand harden and are quickly covered by layers of sediment. After millions of years, scientists find the prints in sandstone, limestone, or shale.

SOUTH AMERICA

DINOSAURS SEEM TO HAVE inhabited South America since their earliest days. Some of the world's most important dinosaurs have come from South America. As in all parts of the world, dinosaur remains are not easily found in areas of dense vegetation. Therefore, in South America most of the remains have been discovered in the near-desert and grasslands in the southeast, in Argentina and in southern Brazil. Dinosaurs have also been found in Peru, Chile, Uruguay, and Colombia. The map (right) shows the major sites. The range of dinosaurs found in South America gives us some idea of the changes throughout the continent's history. Remains of the prosauropod *Riojasaurus* suggest that South America was linked to other continents. Dinosaurs like *Herrerasaurus* are among the most primitive found anywhere. Browsing plant-eaters like the giants *Saltasaurus* and *Titanosaurus* died with all the other dinosaurs 64 million years ago.

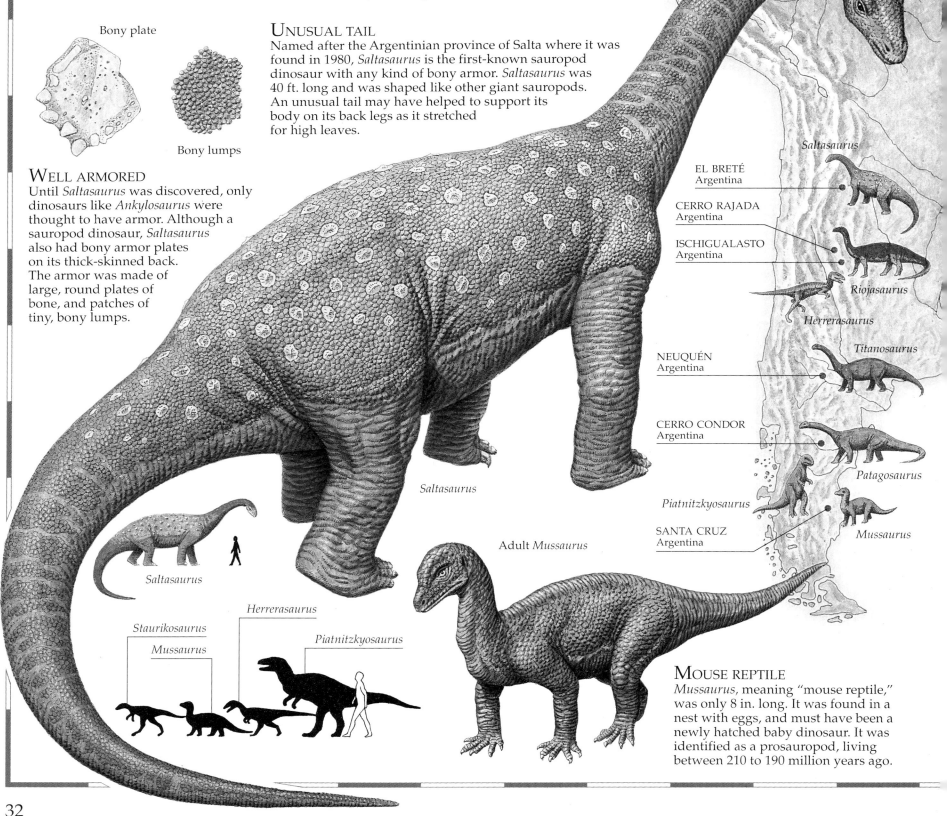

Bony plate

Bony lumps

UNUSUAL TAIL
Named after the Argentinian province of Salta where it was found in 1980, *Saltasaurus* is the first-known sauropod dinosaur with any kind of bony armor. *Saltasaurus* was 40 ft. long and was shaped like other giant sauropods. An unusual tail may have helped to support its body on its back legs as it stretched for high leaves.

WELL ARMORED
Until *Saltasaurus* was discovered, only dinosaurs like *Ankylosaurus* were thought to have armor. Although a sauropod dinosaur, *Saltasaurus* also had bony armor plates on its thick-skinned back. The armor was made of large, round plates of bone, and patches of tiny, bony lumps.

Saltasaurus

Saltasaurus

Adult *Mussaurus*

Staurikosaurus

Mussaurus

Herrerasaurus

Piatnitzkyosaurus

Saltasaurus

EL BRETÉ
Argentina

CERRO RAJADA
Argentina

ISCHIGUALASTO
Argentina

Riojasaurus

Herrerasaurus

Titanosaurus

NEUQUÉN
Argentina

CERRO CONDOR
Argentina

Patagosaurus

Piatnitzkyosaurus

SANTA CRUZ
Argentina

Mussaurus

MOUSE REPTILE
Mussaurus, meaning "mouse reptile," was only 8 in. long. It was found in a nest with eggs, and must have been a newly hatched baby dinosaur. It was identified as a prosauropod, living between 210 to 190 million years ago.

RIOJASAURUS
This dinosaur belongs in the same group as *Massospondylus*, *Plateosaurus*, and *Mussaurus*, but was bigger and bulkier than the first two. A plant-eater, *Riojasaurus* walked on four legs. With a long tail and neck, it reached a length of 40 ft. Although we do not have a skull of *Riojasaurus*, scientists believe it may have been small, like that of its relatives'.

Riojasaurus

Riojasaurus

OLD-TIMER
One of the first dinosaurs, *Herrerasaurus* may be as old as 230 million years. *Herrerasaurus* was a two-legged, meat-eating dinosaur about 10 ft. tall. The dinosaur is so old that it lived before the bird- and lizard-hipped dinosaurs.

Herrerasaurus

THROWING ITS WEIGHT
Between 1977 and 1983 the incomplete fossil skeletons of eight adult and one young *Patagosaurus* were discovered near Cerro Condor on the River Chubut in the Patagonian region of Argentina. *Patagosaurus* lived about 155 million years ago and was a very large, lumbering sauropod dinosaur. It depended on its size and perhaps its long tail for defense.

SANTA MARIA
Brazil

Staurikosaurus

Patagosaurus

Piatnitzkyosaurus

Patagosaurus

SMALL PREDATOR
Also found at Cerro Condor, *Piatnitzkyosaurus* was a predator, and perhaps the slow *Patagosaurus* was its prey. While *Piatnitzkyosaurus* belongs to the same dinosaur family as *Allosaurus*, it was less than half the size of its enormous relative. *Piatnitzkyosaurus* probably behaved like its later, younger cousin.

Staurikosaurus

FAST-MOVING AND HUNGRY
Another of South America's early dinosaurs, *Staurikosaurus* was only 7 ft. long. It would have been a quick and fast-moving predator, on the lookout for careless victims that could easily be caught. After a short, speedy chase, smaller reptiles would be trapped and eaten in its tooth-lined jaws.

EUROPE

THE WORD "DINOSAUR" was first used at a scientific meeting held in Plymouth, England in 1841. It described the three prehistoric, giant reptiles known in Great Britain at the time — *Iguanodon*, *Megalosaurus*, and an armored dinosaur, *Hylaeosaurus*. When dinosaurs first appeared in Europe, the continent was hot and desertlike. *Plateosaurus* was a common inhabitant of this harsh climate. Later, as conditions became more tropical, predators like *Megalosaurus* stalked their prey across southern England. Plant-eaters like *Iguanodon* followed, leaving their remains in many countries. The earliest birds, such as *Archaeopteryx*, lived near warm seas in southern Germany before *Baryonyx* and *Hypsilophodon* appeared. The map shows major dinosaur discoveries in Europe.

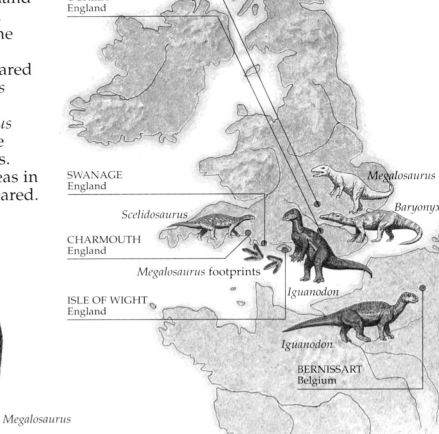

ELGIN
Scotland

STONESFIELD
England

OCKLEY
England

Saltopus

SWANAGE
England

Megalosaurus

Baryonyx

Scelidosaurus

CHARMOUTH
England

Megalosaurus footprints

Iguanodon

ISLE OF WIGHT
England

Iguanodon

BERNISSART
Belgium

Hypselosaurus eggs

TORRES VEDRAS
Portugal

AIX-EN-PROVENCE
France

Camptosaurus

Hypsilophodon

MORELLA
Spain

Megalosaurus jawbone

MAN — OR DINOSAUR?
Megalosaurus was the first of the two-legged meat-eaters ever to be named by scientists. The dinosaur, however, is not very well understood. Not only have its remains been confused with other dinosaurs, but one piece of *Megalosaurus*, the knee-end of its thigh bone, was once thought to be the remains of a giant man! *Megalosaurus* lived about 155 to 145 million years ago. As a predator, its large mouth was lined with daggerlike teeth.

Megalosaurus

REAL SURVIVOR
From its appearance about 150 million years ago, until the extinction of all of the dinosaurs 64 million years ago, the *Hypsilophodon* group was one of the longest-surviving groups of dinosaurs. *Hypsilophodon* itself was a small, fleet-footed plant-eater.

Hypsilophodon

DINOSAUR OMELETTE
A dinosaur-egg omelette — especially coming from *Hypselosaurus* — would have taken a long time to eat. Dinosaur eggs probably did not come any bigger than those of *Hypselosaurus*, whose eggs were 12 in. long and contained 3.5 quarts of fluid. This is as much as 60 hens' eggs, and much tougher to crack!

A REAL FIND

Baryonyx made the news when it was found in 1983, not just because it was a new dinosaur but because it was the most complete example of a meat-eating dinosaur found in Great Britain in this century. Its huge claw was discovered by an amateur collector searching for fossils in a Surrey clay pit.

Baryonyx

Plateosaurus

Plateosaurus

HALBERSTADT
Germany

KELHEIM
Germany

FRICK
Switzerland

Compsognathus

Archaeopteryx

SOLNHOFEN
Germany

Plateosaurus

TROSSINGEN
Germany

Plateosaurus

Compsognathus

NICE
France

SUDDEN DEATH

Remains of *Plateosaurus*, a prosauropod dinosaur, have been found in France, Switzerland, and Germany. The prosauropods were the first large plant-eating dinosaurs, and lived long before the even larger sauropods. Masses of complete skeletons and individual bones of *Plateosaurus* have been found at Trossingen. This could mean that dinosaurs died while migrating across a desert, where they were perhaps drowned by a sudden, storm-fed flood.

The fossilized remains of *Archaeopteryx*, found in Germany.

Archaeopteryx

BIRD OR REPTILE?

Archaeopteryx is one of the most amazing fossils in the world. Only five specimens are known — all from the same limestone rocks in Germany. The rock is so fine that even the outlines of the feathers of *Archaeopteryx* have been preserved. Birds and reptiles are closely related, and *Archaeopteryx* has both the feathers of a bird and the teeth, claws, and tail of the early reptiles.

Plateosaurus   *Baryonyx*   *Archaeopteryx*

Megalosaurus

Compsognathus

35

DINOSAUR MINE

Dinosaur fossils may be found high up on a mountain slope or deep down in a river valley. Many still lie buried under the Earth's surface, and will only be discovered if the rocks above are removed or searchers go underground. This is exactly what happened more than 100 years ago in the village of Bernissart in Belgium when coal miners tunneling underground discovered strange objects. At first the miners thought they had found pieces of fossilized wood, but scientists soon recognized that these were the bones of the dinosaur

Iguanodon. Within a few years more then 39 *Iguanodon* skeletons, many complete, were collected from the deep coal mine before work had to stop because of flooding. *Iguanodon* was a large, plant-eating dinosaur that grew up to 30 ft. long and weighed about 5 tons. The remains of *Iguanodon* have been found in many countries in Europe, and have also been found as far away as North America and North Africa in early Cretaceous rocks 125-110 million years old.

Iguanodon bernissartensis

THE MINE

Above ground, pulleys and wheels turned to raise the coal—and dinosaurs—excavated by the miners working in narrow tunnels below. Earthquakes and underground floods made it very difficult to free the blocks of rock containing the bones.

DIFFERENT DINOSAURS

Not all the *Iguanodon* skeletons from Bernissart are the same. Most are from the same kind, or species — *Iguanodon bernissartensis* — but two are of a smaller, slimmer *Iguanodon*, called *Iguanodon atherfieldensis*. The two kinds are closely related and belong to the *Iguanodon* genus of dinosaurs. Scientists originally thought that *Iguanodon* walked upright on two legs. Now it is thought that they walked on all fours, but may have been able to use two legs as well.

Iguanodon atherfieldensis

LAYERS OF ROCK

The skeletons were found in sandstone and mudstone, which had collapsed among the layers of limestone and coal.

LAYER 1

Most of the *Iguanodon* skeletons were found in a layer 1,056 ft. down, along with fossil crocodiles, fish, and turtles.

LAYER 2

More skeletons were found a few years later, 1,164 ft. down. These were the last dinosaurs to be found in the Bernissart mine.

SIMILAR BUT DIFFERENT

From studying the bones of one type of *Iguanodon*, paleontologists think that this was not just a younger, smaller dinosaur, but a different version of *Iguanodon*. The lightweight *Iguanodon* was first found on the Isle of Wight in southern England. When *Iguanodon* was alive, no sea existed between England and Belgium.

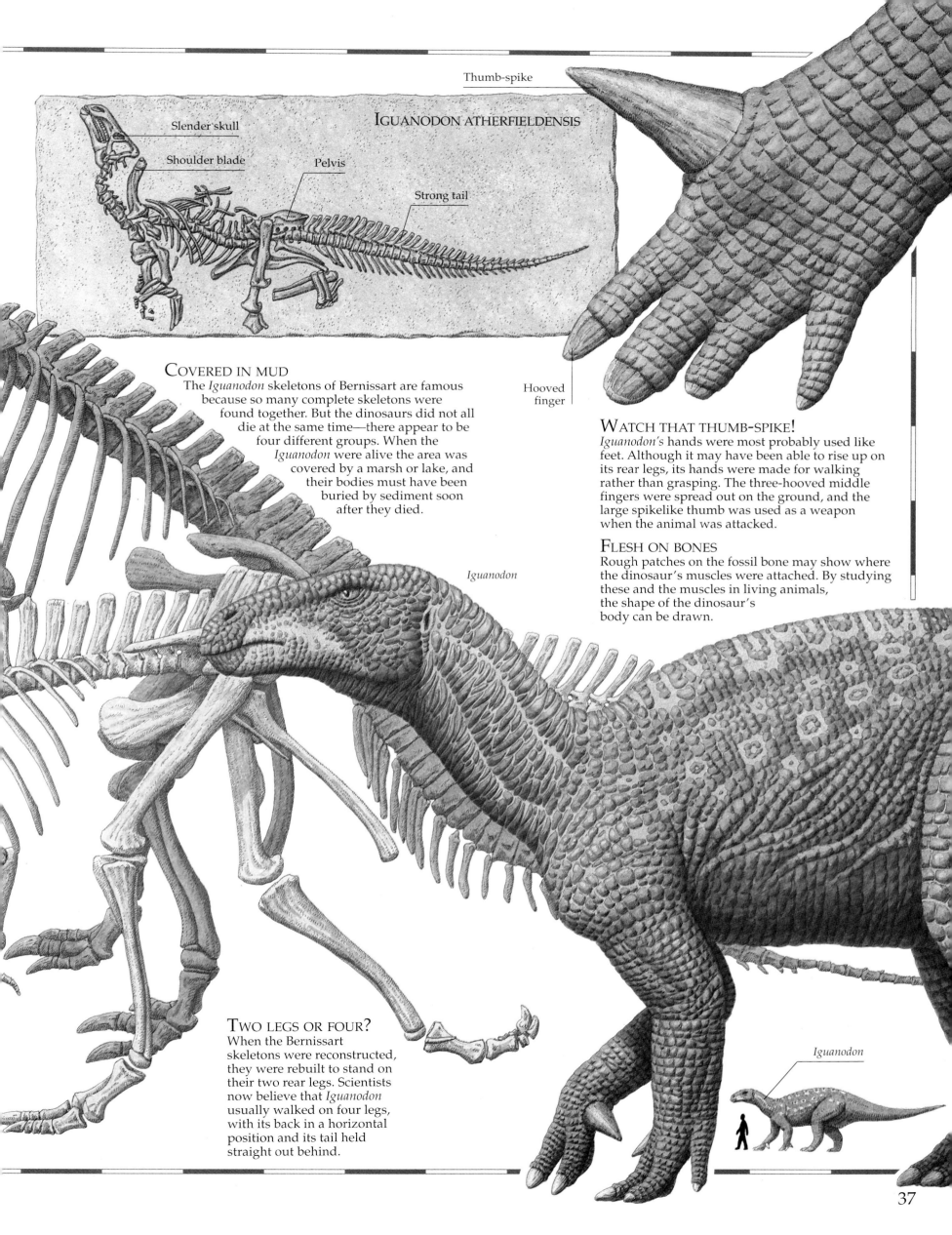

Slender skull

Shoulder blade

Pelvis

Strong tail

Thumb-spike

IGUANODON ATHERFIELDENSIS

Hooved
finger

COVERED IN MUD

The *Iguanodon* skeletons of Bernissart are famous because so many complete skeletons were found together. But the dinosaurs did not all die at the same time—there appear to be four different groups. When the *Iguanodon* were alive the area was covered by a marsh or lake, and their bodies must have been buried by sediment soon after they died.

Iguanodon

WATCH THAT THUMB-SPIKE!

Iguanodon's hands were most probably used like feet. Although it may have been able to rise up on its rear legs, its hands were made for walking rather than grasping. The three-hooved middle fingers were spread out on the ground, and the large spikelike thumb was used as a weapon when the animal was attacked.

FLESH ON BONES

Rough patches on the fossil bone may show where the dinosaur's muscles were attached. By studying these and the muscles in living animals, the shape of the dinosaur's body can be drawn.

TWO LEGS OR FOUR?

When the Bernissart skeletons were reconstructed, they were rebuilt to stand on their two rear legs. Scientists now believe that *Iguanodon* usually walked on four legs, with its back in a horizontal position and its tail held straight out behind.

Iguanodon

BARYONYX

DISCOVERED IN 1983, *Baryonyx* (meaning "heavy claw") is one of the "newest" dinosaurs. Dug out from a clay pit in Surrey, England, the fossil bones were embedded in almost three tons of rock. Some of the bones are still being excavated by the Natural History Museum in London, where the skeleton is being pieced together. It is obvious that *Baryonyx* was an unusual kind of dinosaur. One of the theropod dinosaurs, like *Allosaurus* and *Megalosaurus*, *Baryonyx* was a meat-eater and lived about 124 million years ago. It is the only large meat-eating dinosaur whose remains have been found in rocks of the early Cretaceous period. Since the discovery of *Baryonyx*, scientists have identified similar remains from the Sahara Desert in Africa. These include claw bones and may help us to understand more fully the Surrey *Baryonyx*.

"CLAWS"
This huge claw bone, 12 in. around its outer curve, was the first part of the *Baryonyx* found, giving the dinosaur the nickname "Claws."

TWO OR FOUR LEGS?
Two stout legs were strong enough to carry *Baryonyx*'s weight, but its arms were more robust than those usually found on meat-eaters. Perhaps it used its legs and arms when standing still or walking slowly, and used only two legs when moving quickly.

Baryonyx on four legs

UNUSUAL HEAD
While dinosaurs like *Allosaurus* and *Tyrannosaurus* had short and deep heads, *Baryonyx*'s head was quite different, being long and flat with a small lump on top. A long, very fragile-looking lower jaw gave it an unusual, puzzling shape.

TWO CLAWS ARE BETTER THAN ONE
Only one large *Baryonyx* claw bone has been found, but there were probably at least two. Scientists think the outsized claws were on the inside "finger" of each hand. *Baryonyx*'s arms were quite strong and large, unlike those of other theropods.

Baryonyx

Lepidotes

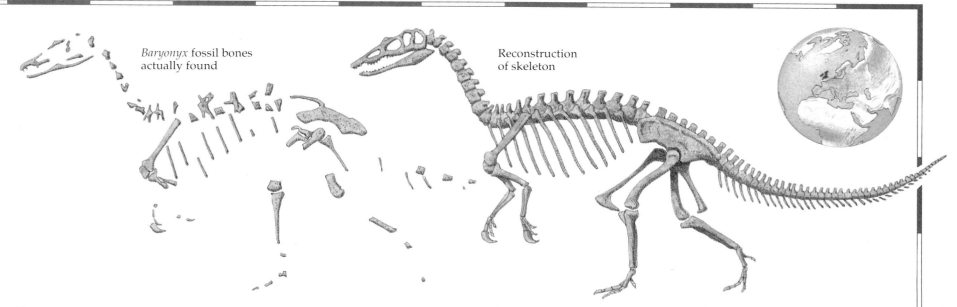

Baryonyx fossil bones
actually found

Reconstruction
of skeleton

Skeleton jigsaw

Less than half of *Baryonyx's* skeleton has been found. Some of its bones may not have been fossilized, while others have been destroyed. What remains is a jigsaw puzzle of pieces.

Clues and guesswork

Because the bones on one side of a skeleton should match those on the other, a copy or model of existing bones can be made. Only a few of *Baryonyx's* tail bones exist, but these are enough for scientists to build a replica.

Hook, line, or claw?

Baryonyx was a meat-eater that may have preferred the flesh of fish to that of land animals. Enormous, hooked claws might have been just what was needed by a dinosaur waiting on a riverbank for a catch. Scales of the fossil fish *Lepidotes* have been found with remains of *Baryonyx*.

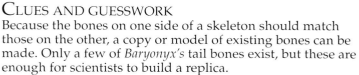

Tail to nose

From its nose to the tip of its tail *Baryonyx* was about 33 ft. long. Its curved neck and muscular body were similar to other large meat-eaters. A few vertebrae and lower spines from the tail are all we have to show that the tail was used to balance the body.

Crocodile smile

Thirty-two sharp, saw-edged teeth lined each side of *Baryonyx's* lower jaw, and there were possibly as many in the upper jaws. The number of teeth, and the curiously curved line of *Baryonyx's* mouth are very similar to those of a crocodile — another reptile well designed for fishing.

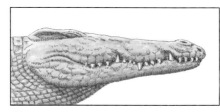

Crocodile teeth

Crocodiles have long jaws lined with many teeth ending at the snout in a wide, toothy fan. Crocodile teeth are sharply pointed, but have no cutting edge. Instead they hold their prey, like slippery fish, and gulp them whole or in large chunks.

Pillar legs

Baryonyx's legs were built like pillars to support its weight. Walking on two legs, Baryonyx would have been almost 13.5 ft. tall. Like other meat-eating dinosaurs, it was probably able to break into a run over short distances.

"Pretty jaw"

AFTER LYING SAFELY BURIED under tons and tons of rock for millions of years, dinosaur bones are exposed for discovery by the forces of erosion. Considering how destructive erosion is, it is surprising that any dinosaur remains can be found today. It is even more surprising when the dinosaur remains that are discovered are from one of the smallest of all known dinosaurs. Only three specimens of *Compsognathus* have been found, and the most complete skeleton measures only 2 ft. 5 in. from one end to the other — about the size of a chicken. This example was found in southern Germany, in the same sort of limestone as *Archaeopteryx*. In fact, the fossil skeletons of the two dinosaurs were at first confused with each other. Some toe bones have also been found in the same area, and a third specimen, about the size of a large dog, has been found in the south of France. *Compsognathus* means "pretty jaw" but with its backward-pointing sharp teeth, it would not have seemed a very pretty sight to the insects and small lizards it caught and ate. As a nimble, speedy runner, 145-million-year-old *Compsognathus* had well-coordinated senses in a world where the bigger dinosaurs ruled.

TINY TERROR
Compsognathus was one of the smallest dinosaurs. Most of the specimens discovered would have been about the size of a chicken, although in life, some may have been larger. *Compsognathus* chased and ate small lizards and insects.

BOOK-SIZE
Not all dinosaurs were giants. The *Compsognathus* shown here is drawn to actual size — hardly bigger than this book!

DEATH POSE
The skeleton here is twisted backward and some pieces have moved apart. When long-necked animals die, their neck muscles and ligaments dry and shrink, causing the neck to curl backward. Gases from the rotting flesh of other parts of the body may cause bones to move apart. Nearly all of the bones have been preserved, but almost half of the tail is missing. Although the dinosaur's head has been turned upside down, the bones around the brain have been fossilized. The back legs are still in place on both sides of the pelvis, and the tiny, sharp, toe bones have hardly changed at all.

LIZARD LUNCH
The bones of another animal were found inside *Compsognathus* — the leftovers of a gourmet meal made of a lizard, *Bavarisaurus*.

READY, STEADY.......
A two-legged runner, *Compsognathus* was able to catch fast-moving insects and small lizards. Its long back legs and long, four-toed feet were essential for providing the speed it needed.

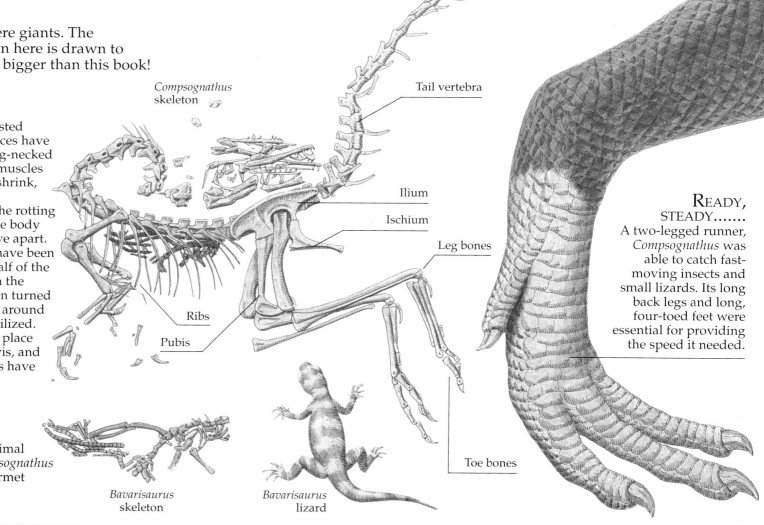

Compsognathus skeleton

Tail vertebra

Ilium

Ischium

Leg bones

Ribs

Pubis

Toe bones

Bavarisaurus skeleton

Bavarisaurus lizard

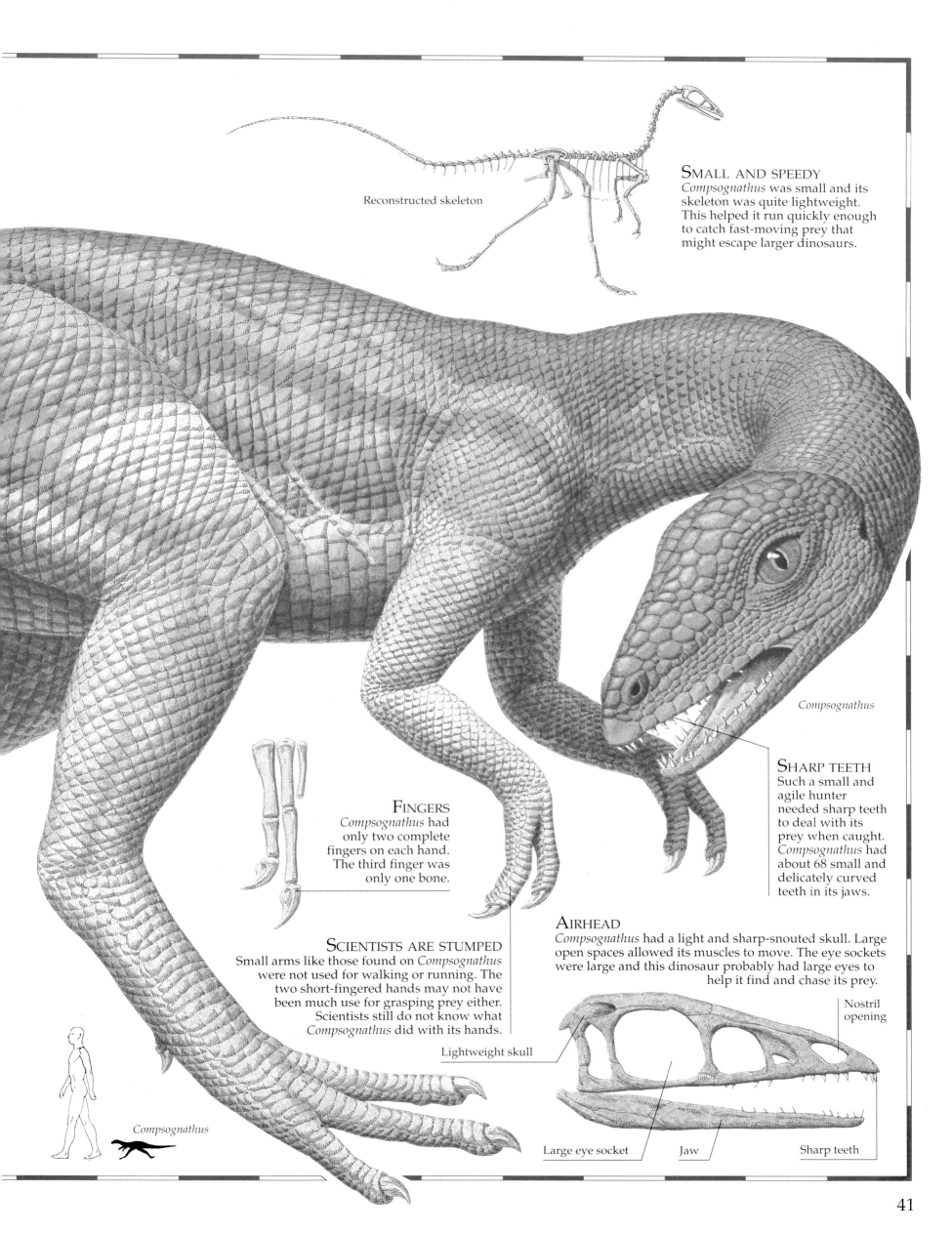

Reconstructed skeleton

SMALL AND SPEEDY
Compsognathus was small and its skeleton was quite lightweight. This helped it run quickly enough to catch fast-moving prey that might escape larger dinosaurs.

Compsognathus

SHARP TEETH
Such a small and agile hunter needed sharp teeth to deal with its prey when caught. *Compsognathus* had about 68 small and delicately curved teeth in its jaws.

FINGERS
Compsognathus had only two complete fingers on each hand. The third finger was only one bone.

SCIENTISTS ARE STUMPED
Small arms like those found on *Compsognathus* were not used for walking or running. The two short-fingered hands may not have been much use for grasping prey either. Scientists still do not know what *Compsognathus* did with its hands.

AIRHEAD
Compsognathus had a light and sharp-snouted skull. Large open spaces allowed its muscles to move. The eye sockets were large and this dinosaur probably had large eyes to help it find and chase its prey.

Nostril opening

Lightweight skull

Compsognathus

Large eye socket

Jaw

Sharp teeth

ASIA

LONG BEFORE DINOSAUR FOSSILS were understood to be the remains of giant reptiles, Chinese people believed they came from dragons. More than 2,000 years ago, these "dragon" bones were thought to have great powers, and they are still used today by some people as medicines. Dinosaurs have been discovered in nearly all of the provinces of China, and "new" dinosaurs are still being found. In Mongolia, expeditions into the desolate Gobi Desert have discovered an amazing variety of dinosaur remains. Since the first dinosaur hunt, undertaken by American scientists in 1922, many expeditions have returned with treasures such as *Protoceratops* and its eggs, "duck bills" like *Saurolophus,* and the *Tyrannosaurus*-like carnivore, *Tarbosaurus*. These finds mean that at some time the Gobi Desert probably had a more hospitable environment. The dinosaurs of India had a separate history from those of the rest of Asia. For much of the age of the dinosaurs, India was a huge island that was slowly moving northward away from its original position between Africa and Antarctica. When the continent "collided" with Asia, it brought its own collection of well-traveled dinosaurs with it. The map (right) shows major dinosaur discoveries in Asia.

TOOTHLESS DANGER
Toothless and only the size of a large dog, *Oviraptor* was a constant threat to its neighbors. Using its strong jaws and two sharp spikes in the roof of its mouth, *Oviraptor* cracked or pierced the eggs of other dinosaurs, draining their contents for a tasty meal. Found in Mongolia by American scientists, *Oviraptor* lived about 80 million years ago.

BUILT FOR SPEED
Looking like a large, featherless ostrich, *Gallimimus* was built for speed. At its fastest it could outrun most other dinosaurs, reaching speeds of 34.5 mph — nearly as fast as a racehorse. A plant-eater, *Gallimimus* also caught insects and lizards.

Titanosaurus

UMRER
India

TIRUCHIRAPALLI
India

Dravidosaurus

TUOJIANGOSAURUS

Tuojiangosaurus must have been one of the most bony dinosaurs that ever lived. Like other stegosaurs it had two rows of bony plates running down its back, and had two pairs of bony spikes at the end of its tail. The plates were once thought to lie flat, covering the back, but this is now known to be wrong. *Tuojiangosaurus* was discovered in southern central China. It lived between 150 to 140 million years ago, about the same time *Stegosaurus* was living in North America. It was a plant-eater, like other stegosaur dinosaurs, with small, weak teeth for snipping off soft shoots and ferns.

Tuojiangosaurus

Oviraptor

Psittacosaurus

Gallimimus

Tsintaosaurus

Tuojiangosaurus

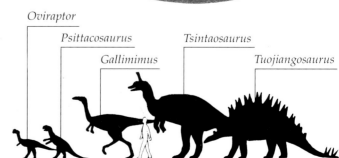

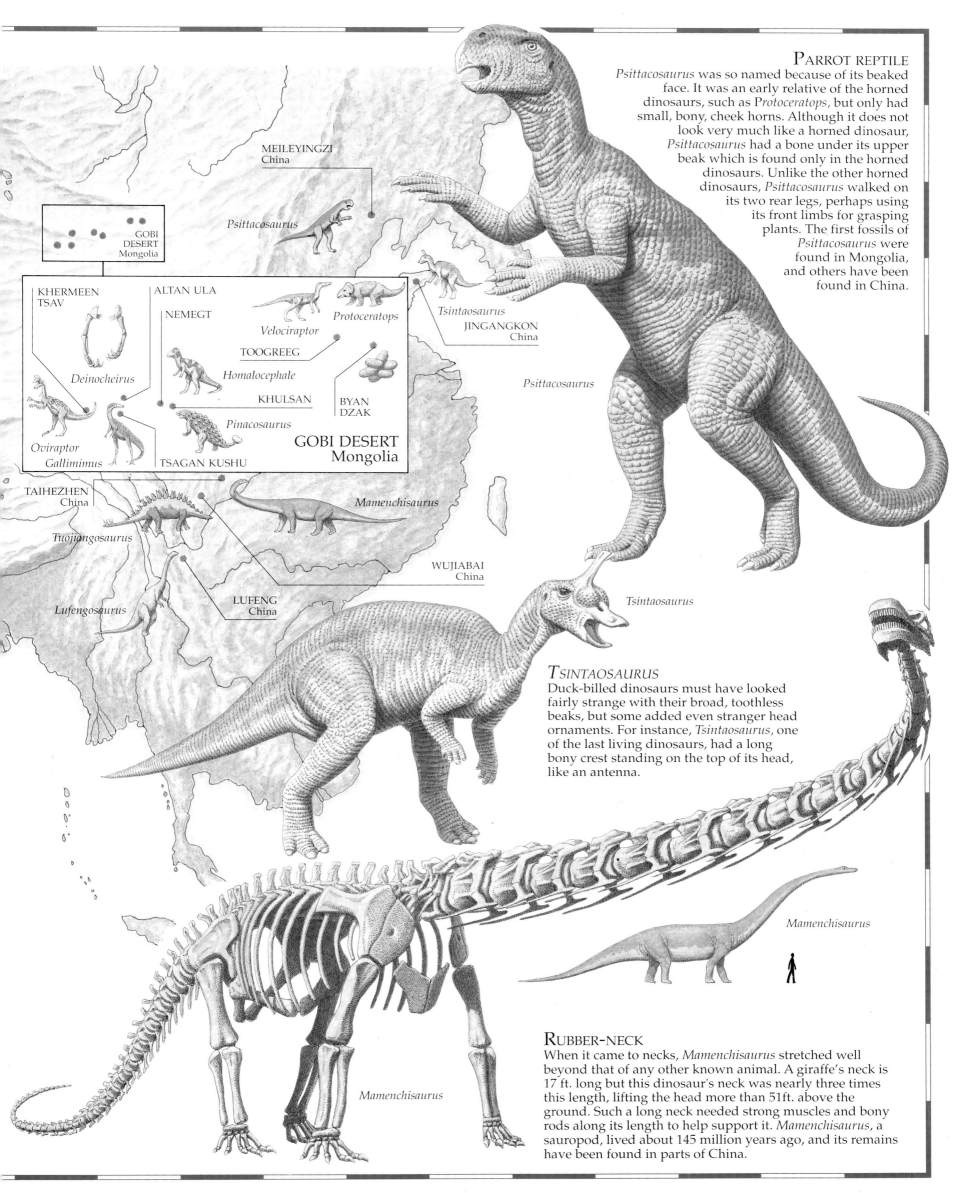

PARROT REPTILE

Psittacosaurus was so named because of its beaked face. It was an early relative of the horned dinosaurs, such as *Protoceratops*, but only had small, bony, cheek horns. Although it does not look very much like a horned dinosaur, *Psittacosaurus* had a bone under its upper beak which is found only in the horned dinosaurs. Unlike the other horned dinosaurs, *Psittacosaurus* walked on its two rear legs, perhaps using its front limbs for grasping plants. The first fossils of *Psittacosaurus* were found in Mongolia, and others have been found in China.

MEILEYINGZI
China

Psittacosaurus

GOBI
DESERT
Mongolia

KHERMEEN
TSAV

ALTAN ULA

NEMEGT

Velociraptor

Protoceratops

TOOGREEG

Deinocheirus

Homalocephale

KHULSAN

BYAN
DZAK

Oviraptor

Gallimimus

Pinacosaurus

TSAGAN KUSHU

GOBI DESERT
Mongolia

Tsintaosaurus

JINGANGKON
China

Psittacosaurus

Tsintaosaurus

TAIHEZHEN
China

Mamenchisaurus

Tuojiangosaurus

WUJIABAI
China

LUFENG
China

Lufengosaurus

TSINTAOSAURUS

Duck-billed dinosaurs must have looked fairly strange with their broad, toothless beaks, but some added even stranger head ornaments. For instance, *Tsintaosaurus*, one of the last living dinosaurs, had a long bony crest standing on the top of its head, like an antenna.

Mamenchisaurus

Mamenchisaurus

RUBBER-NECK

When it came to necks, *Mamenchisaurus* stretched well beyond that of any other known animal. A giraffe's neck is 17 ft. long but this dinosaur's neck was nearly three times this length, lifting the head more than 51ft. above the ground. Such a long neck needed strong muscles and bony rods along its length to help support it. *Mamenchisaurus*, a sauropod, lived about 145 million years ago, and its remains have been found in parts of China.

GOBI DESERT NEMEGT BASIN

THE GOBI DESERT in Mongolia is a vast area of rock and sand, where winds and sandstorms sweep across the mountain slopes and valley floors. In winter the temperature can drop to -104°F, and in summer it might reach more than 113°F in the shade. Several dinosaur hunting expeditions were made into the Gobi Desert between 1963 and 1971. During many months in the desert, some of the best dinosaur remains were found in the Nemegt Valley. Collecting the heavy dinosaur bones was very hard work, and long journeys had to be made for water, both to drink and to make plaster for casting. Some of the bones were partly weathered out of the sandstones and siltstones, and could be dug out close to the surface. Some just needed the sand to be brushed away. The dinosaur bones collected from the Nemegt Valley are still being studied. There are many more waiting to be discovered in this dry and distant land.

HEADLESS BUT RARE

The largest bones found belonged to the sauropod *Opisthocoelicaudia*. Unfortunately, one of the most important parts, the skull, was missing, and there was no neck. Most sauropod dinosaurs lived during the Jurassic period. This find, of late Cretaceous age, is very rare — even without a head.

SUPPORTIVE FEEDING

Unusual tail vertebrae may have helped this dinosaur bend its tail to support itself when feeding.

Opisthocoelicaudia

Deinocheirus' arms compared to the size of a human

Deinocheirus' arms

LONG ARMS

Deinocheirus is a mysterious dinosaur: only its amazingly long arms, 8 ft. long, have been found. No one knows what *Deinocheirus* looked like. It may have been as big as *Tyrannosaurus,* but with longer arms. Who knows what would have happened if the two giants had ever met!

BITS AND PIECES

Deinocheirus was found on a strange day. It was raining. Some of the bones were sticking out of loose sand on top of a small hill when they were spotted. Shoulder bones, arms and claws, and a few scraps of ribs and vertebrae were all lying close to each other — but the rest of the skeleton had not been preserved.

TARBOSAURUS

The first dinosaur found by the expedition was a small *Tarbosaurus*. This dinosaur is so similar to *Tyrannosaurus* that some experts think they may be the same kind of dinosaur, which spread across Asia and North America. So far, at least 13 *Tarbosaurus* skeletons have been found in the Nemegt Basin. The largest ever found on the expeditions was an enormous 40 ft. in length.

A PERFECT FIND

After several days of digging, the almost-complete skeleton of a young *Tarbosaurus* was uncovered, exactly as it had died 80 million years ago.

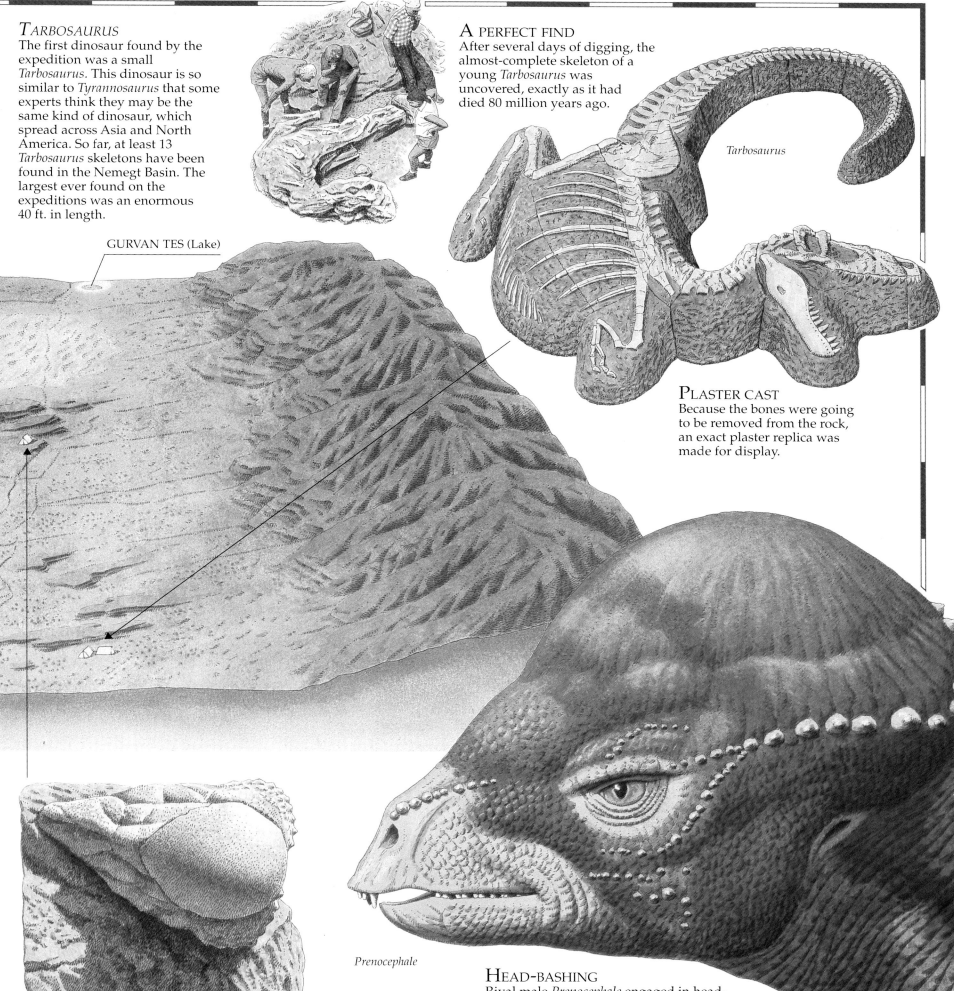

Tarbosaurus

GURVAN TES (Lake)

PLASTER CAST

Because the bones were going to be removed from the rock, an exact plaster replica was made for display.

Prenocephale

EGG-HEADED

The knobby, egg-headed dinosaur *Prenocephale* was discovered in soft sandstone at Nemegt. The inside of the skull is so well preserved that the fine bones of the brain case, with openings for nerves and blood vessels, can be seen perfectly.

HEAD-BASHING

Rival male *Prenocephale* engaged in head-bashing contests to win mates, much as bighorn rams do today. Like a crash helmet, the hard, bony skull of *Prenocephale* would have protected the animal's brain from shocks during these competitions.

HADROSAURS

AMONG THE STRANGEST DINOSAURS, the hadrosaurs, or duck-billed dinosaurs, were also some of the last alive on Earth. Their "duck-bill" nickname comes from their wide, flat, toothless beak, which had a horny cover and was used for biting off twigs and leaves. Strange as it appeared, this beak was quite ordinary when compared with some of the head decorations of the duck-bills. *Tsintaosaurus* had a bony spike sticking up from its skull and some hadrosaurs from North America had trumpetlike crests of hollow bone. *Saurolophus* from China and North America probably had an inflatable balloon of skin over the top of the skull; and some hadrosaurs like *Edmontosaurus* from North America probably had inflatable areas of skin over the nostrils.

These bony crests and blown-up balloons may have been used to "talk" to each other. The inflated skin and bony passages were connected to the nostrils and helped to make loud calls. Also, the shape of bony spikes like the aerial of *Tsintaosaurus* would have been a visual signal to other hadrosaurs. The duck-bills were plant-eating dinosaurs that usually walked on broad-footed rear legs. They first appeared about 100 million years ago, and lived in eastern Asia and western North America, which were probably connected at the time. The hadrosaurs were a very distinct group of dinosaurs. They were probably later relatives of the group that included *Iguanodon*. At 50 ft. long, *Shantungosaurus* may have been the largest of the hadrosaurs.

Shantungosaurus

BIGGEST EVER
Excavated in the Shandong province of eastern China between 1964-8, *Shantungosaurus* was 50 ft. long and may have been the biggest hadrosaur ever. This flat-headed giant of the duck-billed world had large, strong, rear legs. Three "hoofed" toes on each foot spread out to carry its weight.

Saurolophus

BONE-HEADED
Saurolophus lived in Asia and North America from about 75 to 64 million years ago. The Asian animals, like the one shown here, appear to have had longer crests — a prong of bone pointing backward — than the North American *Saurolophus*.

CAN YOU HEAR ME?

Saurolophus with flattened head balloon.

Saurolophus with balloon of skin inflated.

The spiky crests that duck-bills had may have supported flaps of skin on their heads. Between the beak and the crest of *Saurolophus* the skull was flattened on both sides. Here the skin flap lay like an empty balloon. When it was inflated, the stretched pouch would have amplified noises *Saurolophus* made, like the inflated throats of some frogs. This means that dinosaurs must have been able to communicate to each other by making noises.

Tsintaosaurus

REPTILIAN UNICORN
A unicorn among the hadrosaurs, *Tsintaosaurus* from China had a hollow, tubular crest that pointed upward and forward between the eyes. The crest may have supported an inflatable skin flap.

GRINDING AND GRATING
Duck-bills had jaws made for grinding and crushing plants just as cows and horses do. Unlike cows and horses, however, duck-bills did not chew plants by moving their jaws from side to side. Instead, when duck-billed dinosaurs closed their lower jaws against their upper jaws, both sides of the upper jaws were pushed outward in opposite directions, allowing the teeth to grind against each other as the mouth opened and closed.

GRINDING MOUTH
Rows of overlapping teeth, packed into great plant-grinding surfaces, were able to reduce twigs, fruits, and seeds to a soft pulp.

Bactrosaurus

BACTROSAURUS
Bactrosaurus, one of the first hadrosaurs, lived about 95 million years ago. Found in east Asia, *Bactrosaurus* was a small duck-bill, only 20 ft. long. Although it had no head crest, *Bactrosaurus* had vertebrae similar to those of the crested duck-bills, and may have been a relative of these dinosaurs.

Young *Bactrosaurus*

EGGS, NESTS, AND YOUNG

ONE OF THE MOST amazing dinosaur discoveries was made in the Gobi Desert in Mongolia in 1922. There, an expedition of scientists found more than 50 fossil eggs and many skeletons of *Protoceratops* in the desert sandstone. The skeletons were of all sizes, ranging from newly hatched babies to adults. Whole eggs and pieces of broken shell were found in their fossilized sand nest. In one nest 18 eggs were found, and there may have been as many as 34 in the complete nest. This was probably too many for one female to lay, which meant that *Protoceratops* females may have shared nests. These egg, nest, and baby remains were the first real evidence that dinosaurs reproduced like other reptiles.

Oviraptor

Protoceratops

Protoceratops

FEMALES
Although only the hard fossil bones have been preserved, we can identify *Protoceratops* females by the shape of their heads, which had a low frill at the back of the skull and a very small lump on the snout.

YOUNG *PROTOCERATOPS*
Young *Protoceratops* must have been less than 8 in. long when they hatched. As they grew to their full 6 ft., their bony head-frills became broader and taller. These anchored the large muscles that gave *Protoceratops'* jaws the strength to bite tough leaves and plant stems.

Oviraptor

NESTS AND EGGS

Fossil dinosaur eggs have been found in many parts of the world. The largest was about 12 in. long, but the eggs of *Protoceratops* were smaller, only about 8 in. long. Dinosaur eggs were much more elongated than birds' eggs, and the surface of the shell was rough and wrinkled. The shell had many tiny air tubes leading from inside the egg to the outside air, which allowed the dinosaur embryo to breathe. Eggs were laid in circles as the mother turned around in her nest.

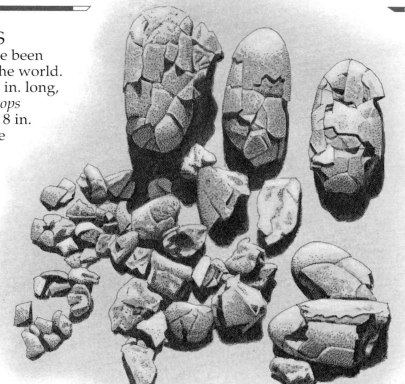

CROCODILE NESTS

Crocodiles are one group of living reptiles that lay eggs. Crocodiles make their nests in sand or from rotting plants. The hard-shelled eggs are then covered over, and the mother stays close to the nest. The young crocodiles have a horny point on their snouts to help them break out of their eggs. The mother clears the sand away, and guards her young as they crawl to the nearby water.

STOP! THIEF!
In one *Protoceratops* nest, the fossil remains of *Oviraptor* were found. Strong, beaked jaws, clawed fingers, and fast-running legs probably made *Oviraptor* a very good egg thief among the nests of *Protoceratops*.

FEND FOR YOURSELF!
After laying their eggs *Protoceratops* females may have left their nests, leaving their young to feed and protect themselves after hatching. Other dinosaurs may have stayed with their babies and cared for them until they were older.

TOUGH EGGS
Inside the eggs the embryos were protected until hatching time. The tough outer shell kept the liquids inside from drying out. This meant that dinosaurs did not have to return to water to lay eggs, like amphibians, and so could spend all their lives on land.

Oviraptor

49

SLOW BUT SUCCESSFUL

THE STEGOSAURS FIRST APPEARED about 160 million years ago. The three stegosaurs shown on these pages — *Tuojiangosaurus*, *Stegosaurus*, and *Kentrosaurus* — all lived between 150-140 million years ago. Fossil bones of stegosaurs have been found in many parts of the world — Africa, North America, China, and Europe. One stegosaur, *Dravidosaurus*, lived in India long after the others had become extinct. *Stegosaurus*, whose name means "roofed reptile," was the first stegosaur to be found. Its name was chosen because its large bony plates were thought to lie flat along its back, making an armored roof. We now believe that the plates stood up to help the dinosaur control its body temperature. Discoveries of many kinds of plated dinosaurs show that although slow plant-eaters, this group of dinosaurs lasted many millions of years.

GROOVED PLATES
On these dinosaurs two rows of bony plates ran down the neck and back to the tail. The triangular-shaped plates stood upright, projecting out from the skin. The bone of the plates is not solid, but is full of spaces; and the surface is covered in grooves. These spaces and grooves were occupied by blood vessels to help control the animal's temperature.

CENTRAL HEATING
Cold-blooded reptiles need to warm up in the sun before they are ready to move into action. They also need to cool down when it is too hot. The bony back-plates of *Tuojiangosaurus* were ideal solar panels and radiators. Sideways to the sun, the blood flowing through the plates spread warmth to the rest of the body. In a breeze or in shade, the plates gave out heat, helping to cool *Tuojiangosaurus* when it was too hot.

Scapula (shoulder blade)

ZIG-ZAG
Scientists think that an alternating pattern of plates in stegosaurs was the most efficient arrangement for heating and cooling the animal.

Tuojiangosaurus

SELF-DEFENSE
The dinosaur's plates were probably too delicate to protect the animal against attack. Instead, it used its long, pointed tail-spikes to keep predators at bay.

Humerus (Upper arm bone)

Tuojiangosaurus

STONES FOR SUPPER
Because *Tuojiangosaurus* could not grind plants with its small teeth, it may have used stomach stones (see p.54) to break up tough plants.

Radius (Forearm)

Ulna

Hand

THICK AND STURDY
Stout, well-jointed front limbs indicate that the dinosaur walked on all fours. Thick, sturdy arm bones were designed to carry the heavy load, and the hands were designed to take the strain of the dinosaur's weight. Five short, broad toes spread its weight over a wide area, and the claws were like hooves.

NOT SO STUPID
Plated dinosaurs like *Tuojiangosaurus* did not have large brains. One stegosaur, *Stegosaurus*, may have had the smallest brain compared to body size of any dinosaur. The brains of plated dinosaurs, however, must have been big enough for their needs, or they would not have been able to survive.

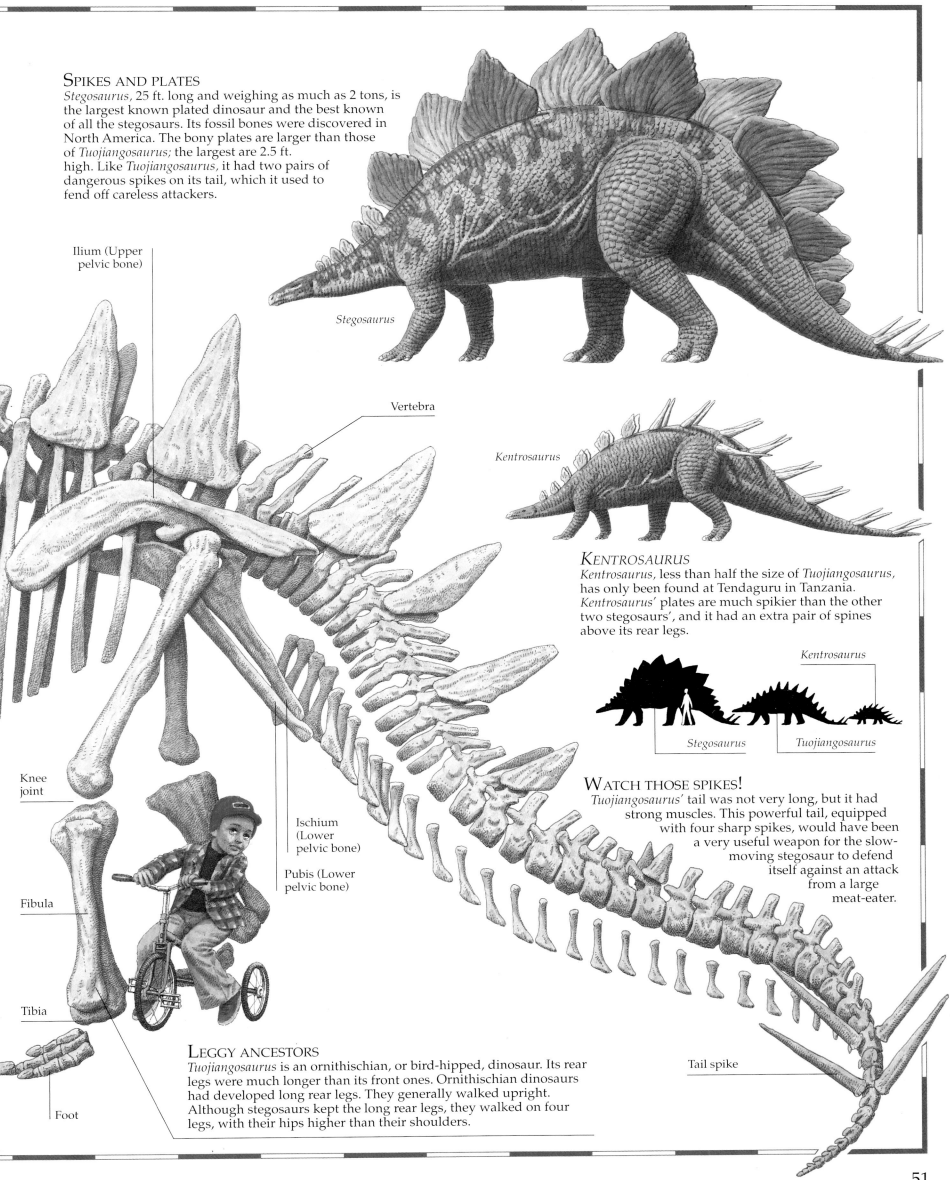

SPIKES AND PLATES

Stegosaurus, 25 ft. long and weighing as much as 2 tons, is the largest known plated dinosaur and the best known of all the stegosaurs. Its fossil bones were discovered in North America. The bony plates are larger than those of *Tuojiangosaurus*; the largest are 2.5 ft. high. Like *Tuojiangosaurus*, it had two pairs of dangerous spikes on its tail, which it used to fend off careless attackers.

Stegosaurus

Ilium (Upper pelvic bone)

Vertebra

Kentrosaurus

KENTROSAURUS

Kentrosaurus, less than half the size of *Tuojiangosaurus*, has only been found at Tendaguru in Tanzania. *Kentrosaurus*' plates are much spikier than the other two stegosaurs', and it had an extra pair of spines above its rear legs.

Kentrosaurus

Stegosaurus   *Tuojiangosaurus*

Knee joint

Ischium (Lower pelvic bone)

Pubis (Lower pelvic bone)

WATCH THOSE SPIKES!

Tuojiangosaurus' tail was not very long, but it had strong muscles. This powerful tail, equipped with four sharp spikes, would have been a very useful weapon for the slow-moving stegosaur to defend itself against an attack from a large meat-eater.

Fibula

Tibia

LEGGY ANCESTORS

Tuojiangosaurus is an ornithischian, or bird-hipped, dinosaur. Its rear legs were much longer than its front ones. Ornithischian dinosaurs had developed long rear legs. They generally walked upright. Although stegosaurs kept the long rear legs, they walked on four legs, with their hips higher than their shoulders.

Tail spike

Foot

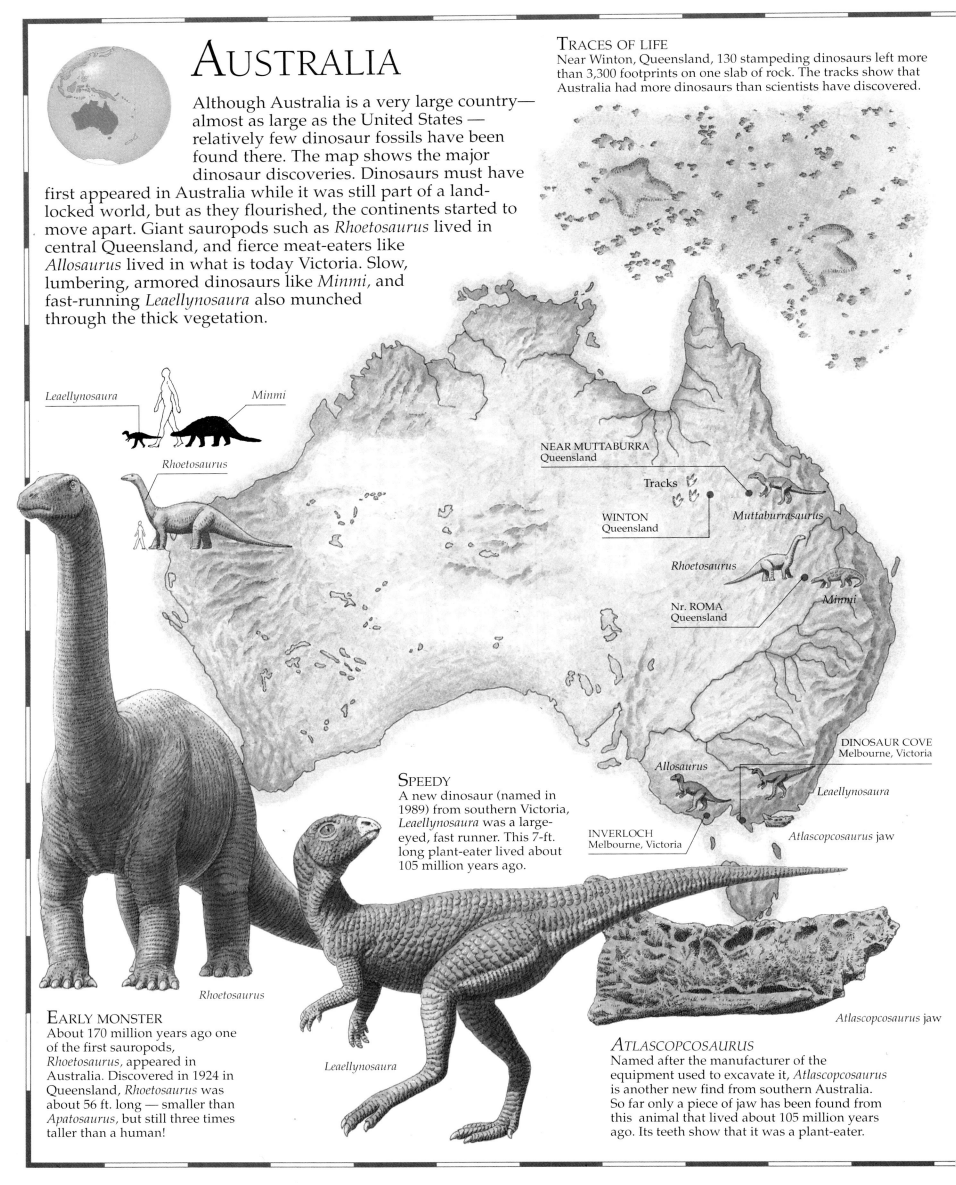

AUSTRALIA

Although Australia is a very large country—almost as large as the United States — relatively few dinosaur fossils have been found there. The map shows the major dinosaur discoveries. Dinosaurs must have first appeared in Australia while it was still part of a land-locked world, but as they flourished, the continents started to move apart. Giant sauropods such as *Rhoetosaurus* lived in central Queensland, and fierce meat-eaters like *Allosaurus* lived in what is today Victoria. Slow, lumbering, armored dinosaurs like *Minmi*, and fast-running *Leaellynosaura* also munched through the thick vegetation.

TRACES OF LIFE
Near Winton, Queensland, 130 stampeding dinosaurs left more than 3,300 footprints on one slab of rock. The tracks show that Australia had more dinosaurs than scientists have discovered.

Leaellynosaura

Minmi

Rhoetosaurus

NEAR MUTTABURRA
Queensland

Tracks

WINTON
Queensland

Muttaburrasaurus

Rhoetosaurus

Nr. ROMA
Queensland

Minmi

DINOSAUR COVE
Melbourne, Victoria

Allosaurus

Leaellynosaura

INVERLOCH
Melbourne, Victoria

Atlascopcosaurus jaw

SPEEDY
A new dinosaur (named in 1989) from southern Victoria, *Leaellynosaura* was a large-eyed, fast runner. This 7-ft. long plant-eater lived about 105 million years ago.

Rhoetosaurus

Leaellynosaura

Atlascopcosaurus jaw

EARLY MONSTER
About 170 million years ago one of the first sauropods, *Rhoetosaurus*, appeared in Australia. Discovered in 1924 in Queensland, *Rhoetosaurus* was about 56 ft. long — smaller than *Apatosaurus*, but still three times taller than a human!

ATLASCOPCOSAURUS
Named after the manufacturer of the equipment used to excavate it, *Atlascopcosaurus* is another new find from southern Australia. So far only a piece of jaw has been found from this animal that lived about 105 million years ago. Its teeth show that it was a plant-eater.

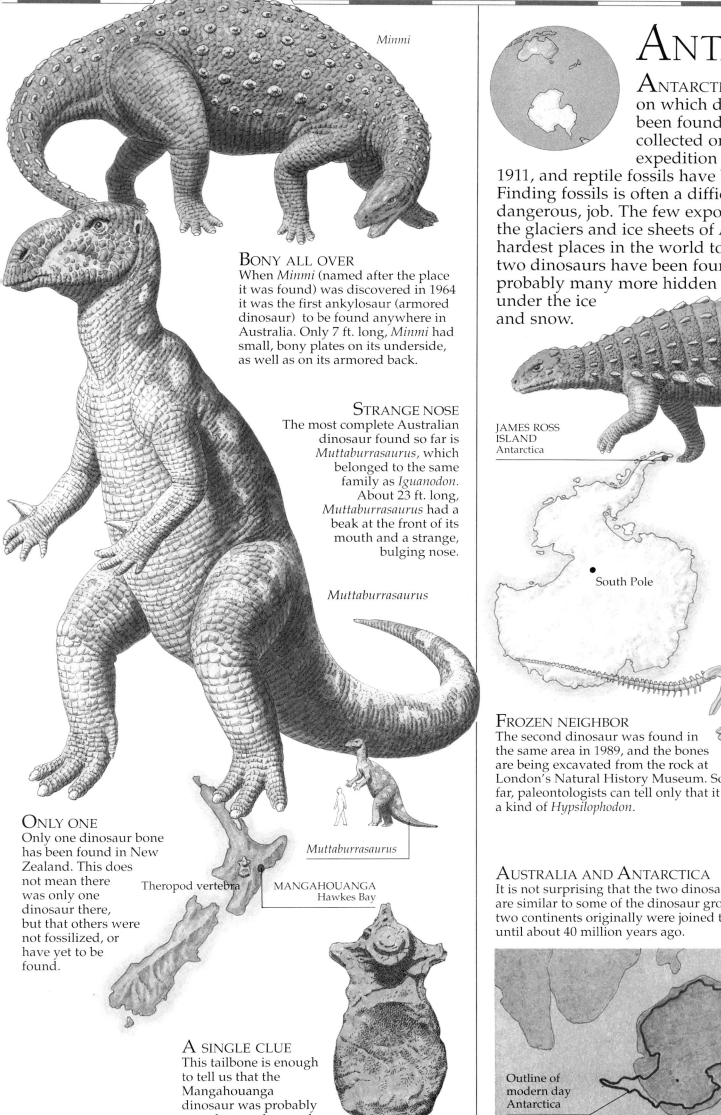

Minmi

BONY ALL OVER
When *Minmi* (named after the place it was found) was discovered in 1964 it was the first ankylosaur (armored dinosaur) to be found anywhere in Australia. Only 7 ft. long, *Minmi* had small, bony plates on its underside, as well as on its armored back.

STRANGE NOSE
The most complete Australian dinosaur found so far is *Muttaburrasaurus*, which belonged to the same family as *Iguanodon*. About 23 ft. long, *Muttaburrasaurus* had a beak at the front of its mouth and a strange, bulging nose.

Muttaburrasaurus

Muttaburrasaurus

ONLY ONE
Only one dinosaur bone has been found in New Zealand. This does not mean there was only one dinosaur there, but that others were not fossilized, or have yet to be found.

Theropod vertebra

MANGAHOUANGA
Hawkes Bay

A SINGLE CLUE
This tailbone is enough to tell us that the Mangahouanga dinosaur was probably a predator, a theropod.

ANTARCTICA

ANTARCTICA is the last continent on which dinosaur fossils have been found. Fossils of plants were collected on Captain Scott's last expedition to the South Pole in 1911, and reptile fossils have been found since. Finding fossils is often a difficult, and sometimes dangerous, job. The few exposed areas of rock among the glaciers and ice sheets of Antarctica must be the hardest places in the world to dig for dinosaurs. Only two dinosaurs have been found so far, but there are probably many more hidden under the ice and snow.

JAMES ROSS
ISLAND
Antarctica

Unnamed ankylosaur

South Pole

NAMELESS ANKYLOSAUR
In 1988 scientists found the first Antarctic dinosaur in the area of James Ross Island. The dinosaur has not yet been given a name, but it is known to be an ankylosaur, an armored dinosaur.

Skeleton of
hypsilophodontid

FROZEN NEIGHBOR
The second dinosaur was found in the same area in 1989, and the bones are being excavated from the rock at London's Natural History Museum. So far, paleontologists can tell only that it is a kind of *Hypsilophodon*.

AUSTRALIA AND ANTARCTICA
It is not surprising that the two dinosaurs found so far on Antarctica are similar to some of the dinosaur groups found in Australia. These two continents originally were joined together, and did not separate until about 40 million years ago.

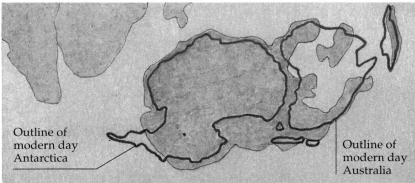

Outline of
modern day
Antarctica

Outline of
modern day
Australia

AFRICA

LONG BEFORE THE FIRST HUMAN ever appeared there, the continent of Africa was home to dinosaurs of all shapes and sizes. In southern Africa, in the ancient Triassic rocks that were laid down more than 200 million years before humans appeared, remains of the prosauropod dinosaurs *Massospondylus* and *Anchisaurus* have been found. In northern Africa, sail-backed *Spinosaurus* has been found in the Cretaceous rocks and sands of the Sahara Desert — formed at the end of the dinosaur age. And in the north and southeast are the giant skeletons of Jurassic plant-eaters like *Cetiosaurus*, *Camarasaurus*, and *Brachiosaurus*. The map shows the major dinosaur discoveries on this vast continent.

Cetiosaurus

Spinosaurus

WAWMDA
Morocco

TAQUZ
Morocco

GADOUFAOUA
Niger

Ouranosaurus

Camarasaurus

IN GALL
Niger

Spinosaurus

DINOSAUR RADIATOR
Living about 100 million years ago, *Spinosaurus*, from North Africa, was one of the huge meat-eating dinosaurs. *Spinosaurus* had all the features of a meat-eater, but it was unusual in one way: along its back, it had a row of enormous spines that held up a sail of skin. This large sail may have been a way of absorbing the sun's rays to warm up, or shedding body heat to cool down. The back plates of *Stegosaurus* probably did the same thing.

Spinosaurus

Gastroliths

GRAVEL GUTS
Eating plants was not a simple task for all dinosaurs. For example, 13-ft.-long *Massospondylus*, a prosauropod, did not have well-designed jaws and teeth for grinding plants. Instead it swallowed stones — called gastroliths — and used these to break up the tough but nutritious parts of plants in its stomach.

Anchisaurus

ANCHISAURUS
With a small skull and long neck, *Anchisaurus*, another prosauropod, was just over half the size of *Massospondylus*. It lived about 195 million years ago. *Anchisaurus* probably use its coarsely serrated teeth to saw through tough stems and leaves.

Anchisaurus skull

Massospondylus

Heterodontosaurus

Lesothosaurus

Massospondylus

Anchisaurus

54

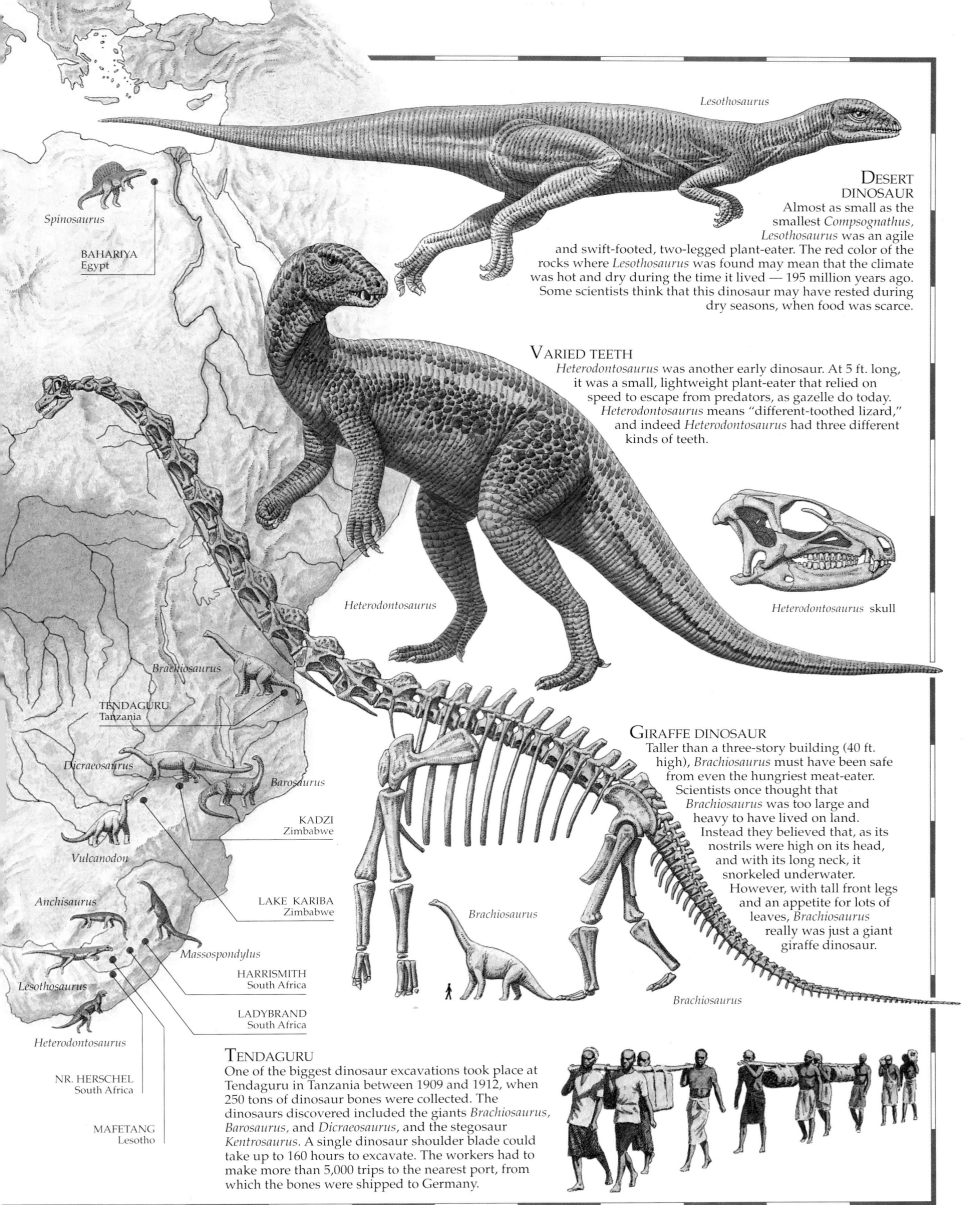

Lesothosaurus

DESERT DINOSAUR
Almost as small as the smallest *Compsognathus*, *Lesothosaurus* was an agile and swift-footed, two-legged plant-eater. The red color of the rocks where *Lesothosaurus* was found may mean that the climate was hot and dry during the time it lived — 195 million years ago. Some scientists think that this dinosaur may have rested during dry seasons, when food was scarce.

VARIED TEETH
Heterodontosaurus was another early dinosaur. At 5 ft. long, it was a small, lightweight plant-eater that relied on speed to escape from predators, as gazelle do today. *Heterodontosaurus* means "different-toothed lizard," and indeed *Heterodontosaurus* had three different kinds of teeth.

Heterodontosaurus

Heterodontosaurus skull

GIRAFFE DINOSAUR
Taller than a three-story building (40 ft. high), *Brachiosaurus* must have been safe from even the hungriest meat-eater. Scientists once thought that *Brachiosaurus* was too large and heavy to have lived on land. Instead they believed that, as its nostrils were high on its head, and with its long neck, it snorkeled underwater. However, with tall front legs and an appetite for lots of leaves, *Brachiosaurus* really was just a giant giraffe dinosaur.

Brachiosaurus

Brachiosaurus

Spinosaurus

BAHARIYA
Egypt

Brachiosaurus

TENDAGURU
Tanzania

Dicraeosaurus

Barosaurus

KADZI
Zimbabwe

Vulcanodon

Anchisaurus

LAKE KARIBA
Zimbabwe

Massospondylus

HARRISMITH
South Africa

Lesothosaurus

LADYBRAND
South Africa

Heterodontosaurus

NR. HERSCHEL
South Africa

MAFETANG
Lesotho

TENDAGURU
One of the biggest dinosaur excavations took place at Tendaguru in Tanzania between 1909 and 1912, when 250 tons of dinosaur bones were collected. The dinosaurs discovered included the giants *Brachiosaurus*, *Barosaurus*, and *Dicraeosaurus*, and the stegosaur *Kentrosaurus*. A single dinosaur shoulder blade could take up to 160 hours to excavate. The workers had to make more than 5,000 trips to the nearest port, from which the bones were shipped to Germany.

REPTILES OF THE SEAS

Ichthyosaurus

WHILE DINOSAURS RULED the land for millions of years, some reptiles chose a life at sea. During the age of the dinosaurs, the marine reptiles like ichthyosaurs, plesiosaurs, pliosaurs, and the turtles were some of the fiercest and largest animals of the world's waterways. Like their reptile cousins on the land and in the skies, the marine reptiles breathed air, which meant they had to come to the surface to fill their lungs. Then they would dive through the water, chasing fish and other sea animals. They hunted these in the shallow waters along the coast, as well as in deep oceans. Reptiles hatch from eggs, and plesiosaurs and pliosaurs probably laid their eggs just as turtles do today. Hauling themselves onto shores with their great flippers they would have scooped out a shallow nest in the sand.

Strangely, although ichthyosaurs were certainly reptiles, they did not lay eggs, but gave birth to live young at sea. Fossil ichthyosaurs have been found with the skeletons of several young animals inside them, or just outside the back end of the body, fossilized at birth. Pliosaurs and plesiosaurs became extinct at the same time as the dinosaurs, but ichthyosaurs died out long before. Turtles still live in water today while their relatives, the tortoises, have returned to the land.

EARLY ACROBATS
With their flippers, fins, and smooth, streamlined bodies, the ichthyosaurs were probably the acrobats of the seas. They first appeared about 220 million years ago, before the dinosaurs, and died out while the dinosaurs continued. Like a dolphin, *Ichthyosaurus* could speed through the waves, diving after squidlike prey while using its "paddles" as rudders for steering.

Ichthyosaurus

Shonisaurus

Archelon

Elasmosaurus

NESSIE
Long-necked plesiosaurs like *Elasmosaurus* fit the descriptions of both ancient sea monsters and creatures like the famous modern-day "Loch Ness monster."

Elasmosaurus

LONG NECK, SMALL HEAD
Plesiosaurs and pliosaurs were closely related, but plesiosaurs had much longer necks and much smaller heads. *Elasmosaurus* was the longest of the plesiosaurs; more than half of its 43 ft. length was neck. Snakelike, it darted its head after fish near the water's surface, catching them with its sharp teeth.

MAKE MINE MOLLUSKS
A small, short-necked pliosaur, *Peloneustes* was only 10 ft. long. Its remains have been found in Western Europe. *Peloneustes*, like other pliosaurs, probably hunted by hiding in wait for its prey and then diving quickly after it. Ammonites — coiled marine mollusks — were a favorite food, and some fossil shells pierced by the sharp teeth of pliosaurs have been found.

THE OLDEST REPTILES
Turtles, one the oldest surviving groups of reptiles, first appeared about 210 million years ago. *Archelon* was a gigantic, almost 14-ft.-long turtle that lived towards the end of the dinosaur period. It may have used its hooked beak to eat shellfish.

Archelon

Peloneustes

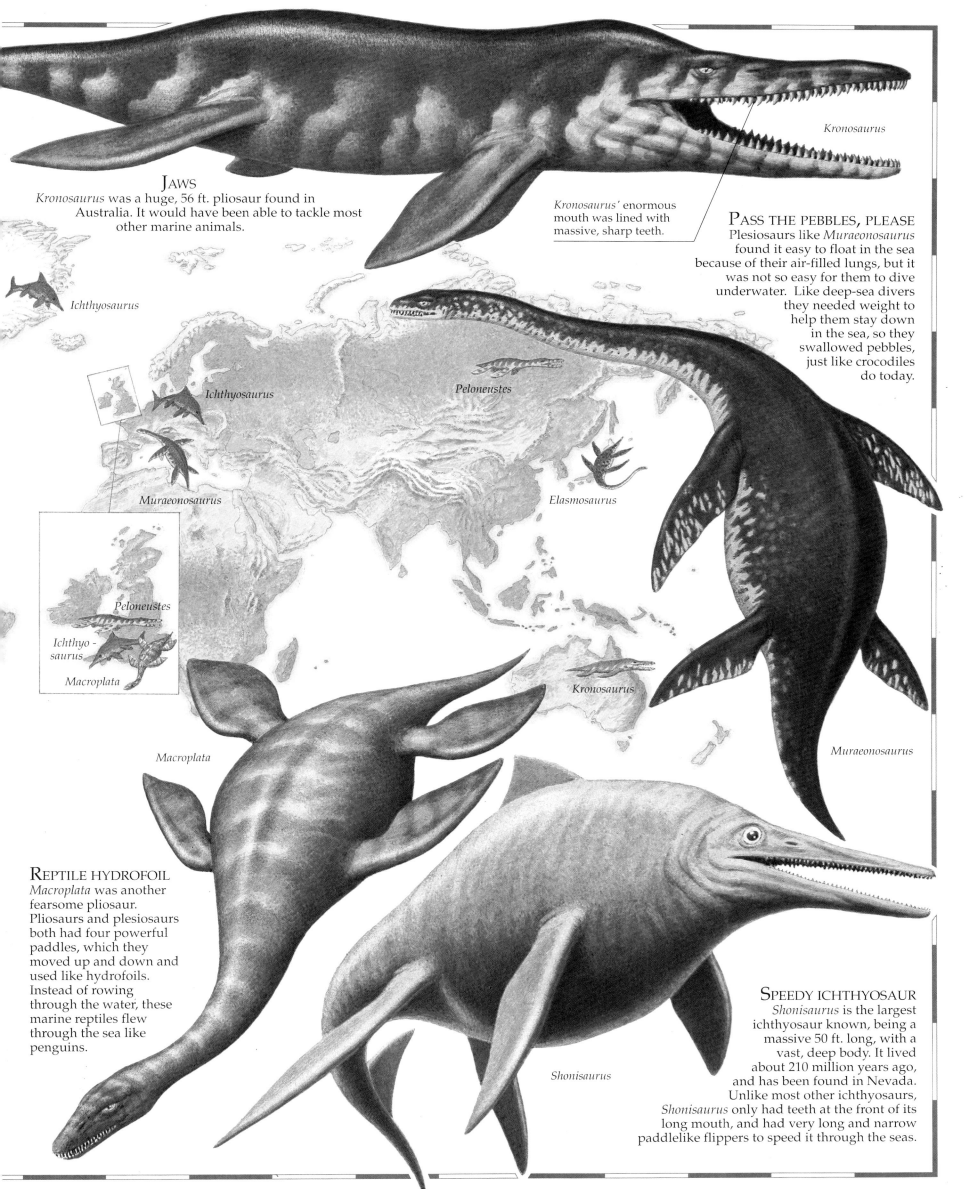

JAWS
Kronosaurus was a huge, 56 ft. pliosaur found in Australia. It would have been able to tackle most other marine animals.

Kronosaurus

Ichthyosaurus

Ichthyosaurus

Muraeonosaurus

Peloneustes

Ichthyo - saurus

Macroplata

Peloneustes

Elasmosaurus

Kronosaurus

Kronosaurus' enormous mouth was lined with massive, sharp teeth.

PASS THE PEBBLES, PLEASE
Plesiosaurs like *Muraeonosaurus* found it easy to float in the sea because of their air-filled lungs, but it was not so easy for them to dive underwater. Like deep-sea divers they needed weight to help them stay down in the sea, so they swallowed pebbles, just like crocodiles do today.

Muraeonosaurus

Macroplata

REPTILE HYDROFOIL
Macroplata was another fearsome pliosaur. Pliosaurs and plesiosaurs both had four powerful paddles, which they moved up and down and used like hydrofoils. Instead of rowing through the water, these marine reptiles flew through the sea like penguins.

Shonisaurus

SPEEDY ICHTHYOSAUR
Shonisaurus is the largest ichthyosaur known, being a massive 50 ft. long, with a vast, deep body. It lived about 210 million years ago, and has been found in Nevada. Unlike most other ichthyosaurs, *Shonisaurus* only had teeth at the front of its long mouth, and had very long and narrow paddlelike flippers to speed it through the seas.

REPTILES IN THE AIR

WHEN THE FIRST FOSSIL pterosaur was found in southern Germany in 1784, it was thought to be of an aquatic animal. This "ptero-dactyle" ("wing-finger") was not commonly accepted as a flying reptile until about 100 years later. The pterosaurs were a group of reptiles that lived at the same time as the dinosaurs. They were related to dinosaurs, but were not dinosaurs themselves. While the dinosaurs had taken control of the land, the pterosaurs made their speciality the air, before birds appeared. Pterosaurs flew on wings of skin, stretched out from their bodies to the tips of their enormously long fourth fingers — their wing fingers. The bones of pterosaurs were remarkably delicate, and full of air spaces to make them light. Their brains were large to enable them to control their muscles and to give them good eyesight. Launching themselves from high points like cliffs, pterosaurs could ride on the updrafts of air, flapping their wings to help their flight. Pterosaurs are divided into two groups, the older "rhamphorhynchoids," and the long-necked, long-headed "pterodactyloids."

REPTILE RUDDER

Eudimorphodon was one of the earliest pterosaurs. Its skull and hind legs may show some similarities with those of the early dinosaurs. It had a short neck and long tail, typical of the "rhamphorhynchoids." This tail, strengthened by extra bony rods, was used as a rudder when flying.

Eudimorphodon

Pteranodon

Quetzalcoatlus

Cearadactylus

Pteranodon

Cearadactylus

FLYING FISH-CATCHER

Pteranodon probably flew over the seas, using its long, toothless beak to catch fish. *Pteranodon* had a wingspan of more than 17 ft. Half the length of its head consisted of a long, bony crest, which may have been used as a rudder to guide and balance the animal while in flight.

COMBING THE SEAS

Discovered in some rocks of the lower Cretaceous period of Brazil, *Cearadactylus* was a large "rhamphorhynchoid" pterosaur. It had a wingspan of almost 13.5 ft., and may have been another fishing pterosaur. Its jaws did not close tightly, and long, curved teeth interlaced between its upper and lower jaws, so that it could comb the sea for fish.

TAILLESS

Pterodactylus was a small wing-fingered pterosaur. Some were as tiny as a sparrow. Like others of its group, *Pterodactylus* had no tail, but had a long, flexible neck. On land, with their wings folded, some pterosaurs may have walked on their sharp-toed feet, while others may have used both their front and rear limbs.

Pterodactylus

LARGEST AND HEAVIEST

The largest pterosaur known, *Quetzalcoatlus* had a wing-span of about 40 ft. The entire animal may have weighed 190 lb., as much as a large human being.

Pterodactylus

Pteranodon

Rhamphorhynchus

Pterodactylus

Sordes

Pterodactylus

Eudimorphodon

Pterodactylus

Rhamphorhynchus

Quetzalcoatlus

Sordes

Rhamphorhynchus

TOOTHLESS BEAK

Many specimens of *Rhamphorhynchus* have been found in southern Germany in rocks of the same age as *Pterodactylus*. Living about 145 million years ago, *Rhamphorhynchus* was similar in appearance to *Eudimorphodon*. However, its slender skull had forward-pointing, spiky teeth with a toothless beak in front.

GOOD INSULATION

Reptiles are normally covered with scales, mammals with hair, and birds with feathers. However, one pterosaur — *Sordes* — seems to have had a thick, hairy coat, which would have helped keep the pterosaur warm during its energetic flights.

MARCHING TO EXTINCTION

DINOSAURS ARE EXTINCT. There are no living dinosaurs, and no human has ever seen one alive. The last dinosaurs died about 64 million years ago. Their fossils are all that is left. During the 150-million-year history of the dinosaurs there were always new kinds of dinosaurs constantly evolving to take the place of the older ones. However, 64 million years ago something very different happened. Not only did the dinosaurs disappear, but with them went many marine reptiles. Other creatures like the ammonites also became extinct, and the flying reptiles—the pterosaurs—suffered the same fate. This mass extinction is made more difficult to explain by the fact that other animals like turtles, fresh-water crocodiles, frogs, birds, and mammals survived the mysterious catastrophe. The disappearance of the dinosaurs was a major change in the animal life on Earth. If dinosaurs had lived, we humans may never have appeared, and large reptiles might still rule.

The ages show, approximately, when each dinosaur became extinct. For some dinosaurs, such as Baryonyx, an extinction date can only be a guess. This is because only one Baryonyx fossil skeleton has been discovered.

Plateosaurus
195 million years ago

Coelophysis
200 million years ago

Massospondylus
198 million years ago

Lesothosaurus
190 million years ago

Heterodontosaurus
180 million years ago

Anchisaurus
185 million years ago

TRIASSIC PERIOD 225-193 MILLION YEARS AGO

Tuojiangosaurus
140 million years ago

Diplodocus
138 million
years ago

Megalosaurus
145 million years ago

Apatosaurus
138 million years ago

Allosaurus
135 million years ago

Ceratosaurus
135 million years ago

Stegosaurus
140 million years ago

Compsognathus
140 million years ago

Baryonyx
120 million years ago

JURASSIC PERIOD 193-136 MILLION YEARS AGO

Diplodocus
138 million years ago

Camarasurus
135 million years ago

Iguanodon
110 million
years ago

Triceratops
64 million years ago

Oviraptor
70 million
years ago

Brachiosaurus
128 million years ago

Deinonychus
100 million
years ago

Baryonyx
120 million years ago

Hypsilophodon
110 million
years
ago

Archaeopteryx
120 million years ago

Protoceratops
75 million years ago

JURASSIC PERIOD 193-136 MILLION YEARS AGO

CRETACEOUS PERIOD

Saltasaurus
64 million years ago

Ankylosaurus
64 million years ago

Tyrannosaurus
64 million years ago

Pachycephalosaurus
64 million years ago

Parasaurolophus
64 million years ago

Gallimimus
64 million years ago

Dravidosaurus
64 million years ago

136-64 MILLION YEARS AGO

STILL A MYSTERY

Perhaps we will never know why the group of animals that had been dominant for 150 million years could not survive. Scientists are baffled by the fact that many groups of animals died out along with the dinosaurs, but others survived. They are not even sure when the dinosaurs began to die out, but we know they disappeared quickly. One explanation is that the Earth received an enormous shock from a colliding meteorite and many animal groups could not survive the sudden changes. Another is that slower changes in the Earth's climate reached a stage where certain groups no longer fitted in. No one has found a complete answer to explain the extinction of the dinosaurs.

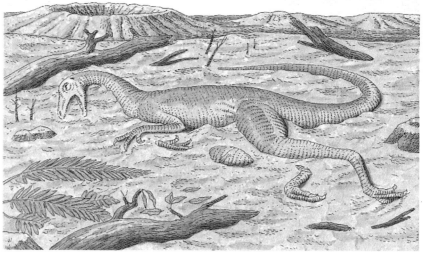

1 DEATH FROM SPACE

Many small meteorites have been found on Earth, and giant craters mark major collisions. The meteorite that may have landed 64 million years ago could have been 5-10 miles wide, and would have made a crater 93 miles wide. The shock of such a crash would have surrounded the Earth in a huge cloud of dust and steam, blocking out the sun for months or even years. Many animals would have been killed by the explosion and the resulting alteration in weather patterns. Dinosaurs may have been particularly vulnerable to these changes in the ecology of the Earth. Other animals, however, were able to survive this crisis and populate new areas.

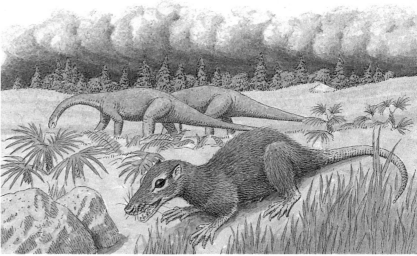

2 SLOWLY CHANGING

The extinction of the dinosaurs and other animal groups may not have been so sudden. The Earth is constantly changing as continents move and are altered. By 64 million years ago the continents had separated extensively. Some seas had spread into the continents, and there was generally a higher sea level across the world. The Earth's weather became cooler. Tropical climates became limited, and many of the plants that grew there were replaced by more modern ones. These slow changes may have been too much for the dinosaurs, and their place as rulers of the world was taken over by the mammals.

Index

Acknowledgments

Dorling Kindersley would like to
thank Mandy Earey for design
assistance and Lynn Bresler for
compiling the index